IN GERMANY

Rod Nash

About this book

In Germany gives insight into the everyday life and culture of the German-speaking people of Europe. Although it concentrates on Germany, references are also made to Austria and Switzerland.

Language

There is plenty of useful language within the book, particularly the German you might need when visiting a German-speaking country. This book will be of most help to you if you already know a little German. The book is designed so that information is given in English, but photo captions and relevant vocabulary (with a translation) are in German. There are various language activities and practice sessions under the heading **Übung macht den Meister** (Practice makes perfect).

Meike, Matthias and Daniel

Meike and Matthias are German teenagers who tell us a lot about their country. Daniel is a visitor to Germany, who asks many of the questions you would probably like to ask.

For Laura and Daniel

Editor: Sue Chapple
Designer: Wendi Watson
Language advisor: Sonja Osthecker
Cartoonists: David Parkins and David Lock

ISBN 0-905703-99-5

© Chancerel International 1991
PN 4 3 2 / 1996 1995

All rights reserved. No part of this publication may be reproduced, recorded, transmitted or stored in any retrieval system, in any form whatsoever, without the written permission of the copyright holders.

Chancerel International Publishers
40 Tavistock Street
London WC2E 7PB

Printed in Hong Kong

Inhalt

Willkommen!	4	Im Café	44
Was weißt du über Deutschland?	6	Wir gehen einkaufen	46
Ein bißchen Geschichte	8	Im Kaufhaus	48
Die friedliche Revolution	10	Souvenirs zum Mitnehmen	50
Wie kommt man nach Deutschland?	12	Auf der Post	52
Was soll ich mitnehmen?	14	In der Stadt	54
Es gibt so viel zu sehen	16	Ein Spaziergang durch eine deutsche Großstadt	56
Zwei Hauptstädte	18	Was gibt's zu sehen?	58
Einige Städte	20	Wir bleiben zu Hause	60
Hinaus in die Natur	22	Wir gehen aus!	62
Im Hotel	24	Vielen Dank für die Einladung	64
Wo kann ich billig übernachten?	26	So viele Schilder ... und Reklamen	66
Ein deutsches Haus	28	Noch mehr Schilderwald	68
In einer deutschen Familie	30	In einer deutschen Schule	70
Auf der Straße	32	Mehr über deutsche Schulen	72
Straßenschilder und Verkehrszeichen	34	Hilfe!	74
An der Tankstelle	36	Pressemeldungen	76
Mit der Bahn unterwegs	38	Letzte Eindrücke	78
Wir gehen essen	40		
In der Imbißstube	42		

Photographs: Front cover: Spectrum Colour Library (Freiburg); Back cover: Frankfurt Tourist Office; Helga Holtkamp (Berlin); ADAC 32, 33; Allsport 75; Austrian National Tourist Office 19; Bundesbildstelle 13; Bundesministerium für das Post- und Fernmeldewesen 50; Deutsche Bundesbahn 36, 37; Deutsches Jugendherbergswerk 24, 25; Bob Hallmann 56, 62, 65; Helga Holtkamp 22, 26, 43; Inter-Nationes 15, 16, 19, 28, 38, 69; Karstadt 49; Kaufhof 46; Lufthansa 12; Gerd Mothes/Gewandhaus zu Leipzig 74; Press Association 74; Jürgen Schadeberg 9, 48; Sporting Pictures 7; Tony Stone 23; David Streeter 23; Swiss National Tourist Office 18; Tourismus-Zentrale Hamburg GmbH 18; Verkehrsamt Frankfurt 54, 55; Mike Watson 14.

All remaining photographs by Rod and Sonja Nash.

Every effort has been made to contact copyright holders. We apologise if any have been overlooked.

Willkommen!

Die Kaiser-Wilhelm-Gedächtniskirche in Berlin

◀ *Die Wartburg in Eisenach*

Der Spessart östlich von Frankfurt

◀ *Der Marktplatz in Bremen*

Baden-Württemberg	
Einwohner	9,4 Millionen
Hauptstadt	Stuttgart
Bayern	
Einwohner	11,0 Millionen
Hauptstadt	München
Berlin	
Einwohner	3,4 Millionen
Hauptstadt	Berlin
Brandenburg	
Einwohner	2,7 Millionen
Hauptstadt	Potsdam
Bremen	
Einwohner	0,66 Millionen
Hauptstadt	Bremen
Hamburg	
Einwohner	1,6 Millionen
Hauptstadt	Hamburg
Hessen	
Einwohner	5,6 Millionen
Hauptstadt	Wiesbaden
Mecklenburg-Vorpommern	
Einwohner	2,1 Millionen
Hauptstadt	Schwerin
Niedersachsen	
Einwohner	7,2 Millionen
Hauptstadt	Hannover
Nordrhein-Westfalen	
Einwohner	16,9 Millionen
Hauptstadt	Düsseldorf
Rheinland-Pfalz	
Einwohner	3,7 Millionen
Hauptstadt	Mainz
Saarland	
Einwohner	1,1 Millionen
Hauptstadt	Saarbrücken
Sachsen	
Einwohner	4,9 Millionen
Hauptstadt	Dresden
Sachsen-Anhalt	
Einwohner	3,0 Millionen
Hauptstadt	Magdeburg
Schleswig-Holstein	
Einwohner	2,6 Millionen
Hauptstadt	Kiel
Thüringen	
Einwohner	2,5 Millionen
Hauptstadt	Erfurt

Was weißt du über Deutschland?

Guten Tag!

Guten Tag! Ich heiße Meike, und ich wohne in Dortmund. Ich werde dir viel über mein Land erzählen und auch etwas über andere Länder, wo man Deutsch spricht. Kennst du einige dieser Länder?

Hallo! Ich heiße Matthias, und ich bin Meikes Freund. Ich wohne auch in Dortmund. Kannst du Dortmund auf einer Karte finden? Es liegt im östlichen Ruhrgebiet; das ist ein großes Industriegebiet in Deutschland.

Hi! I'm Daniel! I learn German at school. I'm going to Germany soon so I must start getting organised. I'm really excited!

Eine Fußgängerzone in Dortmund

Ein Quiz

Let's see what you already know.

1 Here are the four countries where German is spoken, and their capital cities. Which capital belongs to which country?

Land	Hauptstadt
Deutschland	Wien
Österreich	Berlin
Schweiz	Vaduz
Liechtenstein	Bern

2 Here are the four flags of the countries in question 1. Which flag belongs to which country?

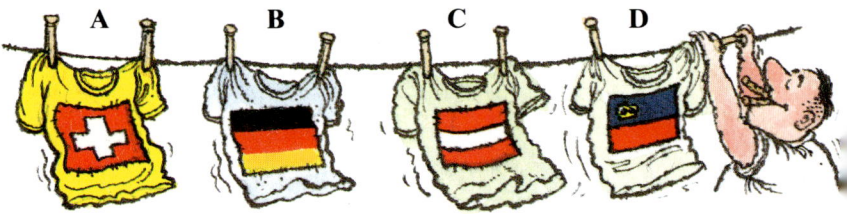

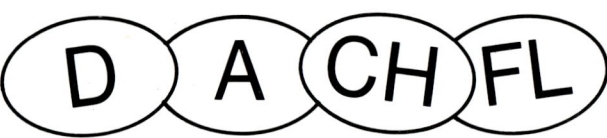

3 Here are the international registration plates of the four countries. Which plate belongs to which country?

4 Here are some famous sports personalities from German-speaking countries. Who does which sport, and from which country does each of them come?

Steffi Graf
Gerhard Berger
Lothar Matthäus
Petra Kronberger
Bernhard Langer
Katrin Krabbe

A Fußball
B Golf
C Tennis
D Leichtathletik
E Autorennnen
F Skifahren

Boris Becker ist ein Tennisspieler. Er hat schon mehrere Male Wimbledon gewonnen. Weißt du, in welchem Jahr er zum ersten Mal gewonnen hat? Wie alt war er?

Nicht vergessen!

Things to remember when you are in Germany

DO remember that cars drive on the right.

DO wait at pedestrian crossings until your light is green. You can be fined on the spot if you are caught crossing when the light is red.

DO try lots of different foods and drinks. This boy is trying **Wiener Backhendl** (chicken baked in bread crumbs). Would you like to try it yourself?

DO write down new words and phrases. Try and write them down in the context you heard or read them; this will help you to remember them.

DO speak as much German as you can. Nobody minds if you make mistakes.

DO collect things for a souvenir album – for example, tickets, stamps, postcards, brochures, beer mats, wrappers.

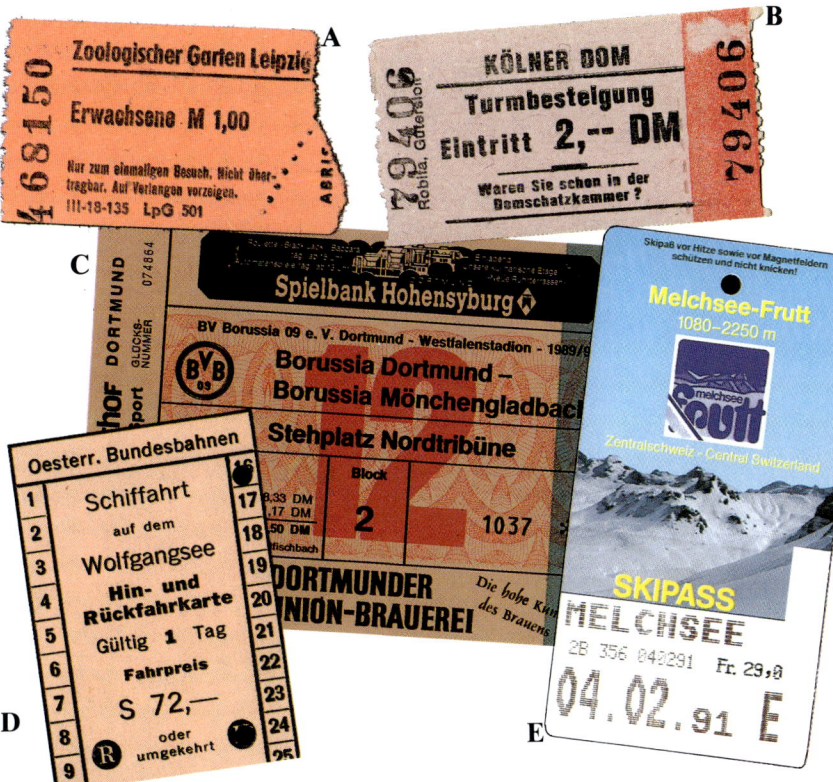

1 Which of these tickets is for:
   a) a soccer match?
   b) a boat ride on a lake?
   c) a visit to the zoo?
   d) climbing up a cathedral?
   e) skiing?

2 Which countries are these tickets from?
3 Which currencies are mentioned?
4 Which currency no longer exists?

Ein bißchen Geschichte

Deutschland nach dem Zweiten Weltkrieg

At the end of World War II, Germany and Austria were divided into four zones, each zone being occupied by one of the victorious allied powers – France, Britain, the United States and the Soviet Union. The German capital Berlin, situated well inside the Soviet zone, was similarly divided into four sectors.

In May 1949, the three Western zones became **die Bundesrepublik Deutschland** (the Federal Republic of Germany), with Bonn as its capital and Konrad Adenauer as its first **Bundeskanzler** (Federal Chancellor). The Soviet zone had gone its own political and social way, and in the same year it became part of the Communist bloc as **die Deutsche Demokratische Republik** (the German Democratic Republic). One year earlier, the isolated city of West Berlin had become the heart of the Cold War when the Soviet Union tried to cut it off from the Western World with a year-long blockade, which was eventually abandoned.

Austria became an independent republic again in 1955, when the occupying forces withdrew.

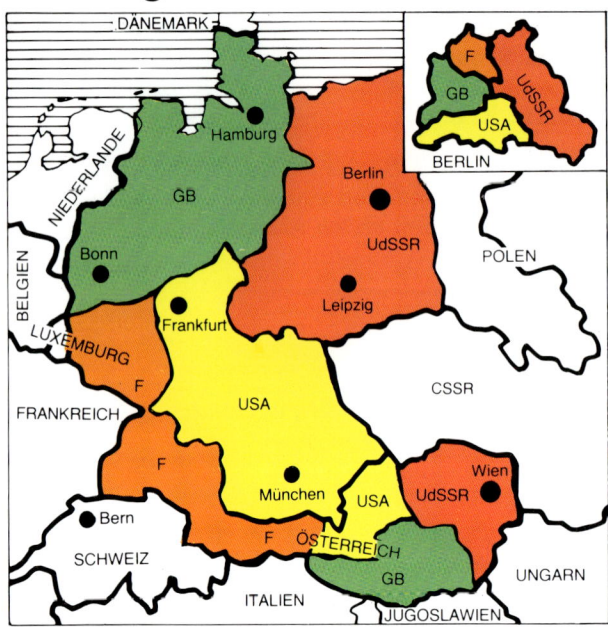

Eine Landkarte des geteilten Deutschlands

Das Wirtschaftswunder

After the war, the Western Allies were determined to help West Germany to recover. The currency reform of 1948, the dollars provided by the American Marshall Plan, and last but not least the determination of the West German people, sparked off the **Wirtschaftswunder** (Economic Miracle) that made West Germany into one of the most prosperous countries of the world. The economic expansion was helped by the so-called **Gastarbeiter** (guest workers) from Southern Europe, who came to do much of the manual work in factories and on the roads, as well as opening restaurants and shops. In 1988 there were about 4·5 million **Gastarbeiter** in Germany.

Die politischen Parteien

The Germans have two votes, one for a local candidate and one for a political party. Thus half of the **Bundestag** (the equivalent of our House of Commons) is elected by proportional representation. A party has to get 5% of the national vote before it can send **Abgeordnete** (Members of Parliament) to the **Bundestag** – this is intended to ensure that candidates from an extreme political party cannot be elected.

The main political parties are:
CDU: Christlich-Demokratische Union (Conservatives)
CSU: Christlich-Soziale Union (Bavarian equivalent of the CDU)
SPD: Sozialdemokratische Partei Deutschlands (Labour)
FDP: Freie Demokratische Partei (Liberals)
Die Grünen (The Greens; an ecology party)
PDS: Partei des Sozialistischen Fortschritts (a party which emerged from the **Sozialistische Einheitspartei Deutschlands (SED)** which once ruled the German Democratic Republic)
Die Republikaner (right wing republican party, founded in 1987).

Beispiele von politischen Parolen in der ehemaligen DDR

Die Deutsche Demokratische Republik

Industry revived here too, but much more slowly. Dissatisfaction with the system was rife, and in June 1953, when work quotas were increased, the people of East Berlin went out on the streets to protest. The revolt was crushed by Soviet tanks, and an estimated 400 people lost their lives. Thousands then left the GDR in the following years, until in 1961 the East Germany Government stopped the flood of refugees by building the Berlin Wall. With the border between the two Germanies also protected by an "iron curtain" of watch towers, mines, barbed wire and soldiers, escape to the West became a hazardous task which only few people would dare risk. The division of Germany seemed complete.

Das Leben in der DDR

With the manufacture of many items under state control, there was little competition and no need for advertising. Any signs around a town tended to be political slogans in praise of Communism.

Though basic foodstuffs and accommodation remained very cheap in the GDR, other items, such as coffee and imported fruit, were considered luxuries and were extremely expensive and hard to get. Moreover, Western television provided the East Germans with evidence of the ever-rising standard of living in the West. They saw the packed stores and the new and numerous cars. Even more distressing was the lack of freedom – the right to criticise the State and to travel to the West.

In 1966, 28 per cent of Germans thought it was unlikely that East and West Germany would ever be united again. In 1980, 80 per cent held that view. Then came 1989...

Below are the results of the 1990 election to the **Bundestag**.

Parteien	Zweitstimmen		Prozent
CDU	17 051 128	=	36,7
SPD	15 539 977	=	33,5
FDP	5 123 936	=	11,0
CSU	3 301 239	=	7,1
GRÜNE	1 788 214	=	3,9
PDS	1 129 290	=	2,4

Die Wahl zum Deutschen Bundestag 1990

Oben: Grenzübergang Checkpoint Charlie
Unten: Ein DDR-Soldat springt in die Freiheit.

Die friedliche Revolution

Der 9. November 1989

On the evening of November 9, 1989, thousands of East Germans flooded past bewildered border guards into West Berlin. People from East and West fell into each other's arms, danced on the Wall and couldn't believe their eyes. The unimaginable had happened – the seemingly impregnable Berlin Wall had opened, and the days of a divided Germany were numbered. How did all these dramatic changes come about?

There is no doubt that changes in the Soviet Union and the more liberal policies of the Soviet leader Mikail Gorbachov triggered a series of events that, via Hungary and Czechoslovakia, led to the collapse of the border between East and West Germany. Of initial importance was Hungary's step to open its borders to Austria and to allow East German citizens to leave, without having first consulted with East Berlin. This is how West German newspapers reported events from September 1989 onwards:

Ungarns Grenzen für DDR-Bürger geöffnet

Sonntag, den 10.9.89
Hungary's borders are opened to citizens of the GDR.

Mit Vollgas in die Freiheit:

Montag, den 11.9.89
"Full throttle into freedom."
East Germans take their Trabi cars to the Austro-Hungarian border.

Die Lage in Prag wird unerträglich

Freitag, den 29.9.89
The situation in Prague becomes unbearable as 3000 East Germans take refuge in the Federal Republic's Embassy. Finally the West German Foreign Minister, Hans-Dietrich Genscher, negotiates their departure to the West.

Größte Demonstration der DDR-Geschichte

Montag, den 16. Oktober
The largest demonstration in East Germany's history takes place as 120,000 people call for reform.

Erich Honecker entmachtet

Mittwoch, den 18. Oktober
Erich Honecker, the GDR's long-time leader, loses power.

„Wir fordern freie Wahlen"
Rund eine Million DDR-Bürger gingen in Ost-Berlin auf die Straße

Sonntag, den 5. November
About a million people take to the streets of East Berlin, demanding free elections. Now Czechoslovakia, too, has opened its borders to the West, and thousands are still fleeing every day.

DDR öffnet ihre Grenzen für alle

Donnerstag, den 9. November
The GDR opens its borders for all citizens.

Samstag/Sonntag, 11./12. November 1989
A weekend of "borderless" (unbounded) freedom.

Wochenende grenzenloser Freiheit

How ironic that a wall that had been built to stop people escaping, has now been opened for effectively the same reason!

Der Weg zur Wiedervereinigung

The communist SED continued to govern East Germany until March 1990, when the first free election ever in the GDR took place. Left-wing parties like **Neues Forum** (New Forum), which had played a leading part in bringing about the changes in the GDR, were swept aside, and the conservative CDU under Lothar de Maizère won the day – an obvious cry for the **Marktwirtschaft** (market economy) that made the West prosperous in comparison.

Meanwhile Helmut Kohl, the West German **Bundeskanzler**, had been negotiating all the time with the occupying powers for a united Germany. On July 1, 1990 the East German mark ceased to exist, and the West German mark became the currency for both countries. When West Germany agreed to recognize once and for all the Oder-Neiße line between Poland and Germany, the way was open for official unification on October 3, 1990.

Hier hämmern Souvenir-Jäger an der Mauer – aber früher spielten sich hier viele Tragödien ab. Noch im Februar 1989 wurde an dieser Stelle ein Flüchtling erschossen.

Die ersten Probleme

Inevitably there were many problems ahead: as state subsidies were abolished, the cost of living rose steeply in the East; unemployment, too, increased sharply while there was a disappointing lack of investment by Western companies in the East. There were severe environmental problems in the East, and the cost of unification put a strain on West Germany's economy as well as causing housing shortages with so many East Germans having fled or now moving to the West.

On December 3, 1990, the CDU won the first elections held in the newly united Germany, although 1991 saw them lose a great deal of popularity. The process of re-building a united Germany continues; on June 20, 1991, the decision was taken to return the seat of government from Bonn to Berlin.

Ein ostdeutscher "Trabi" – für viele ein Symbol der friedlichen Revolution – steht zusammen mit westlichen Autos vor dem Reichstag. Der Reichstag wird bald wieder Sitz der deutschen Regierung sein.

Die Hochzeit des Jahres: Ein Westberliner und seine Ostberliner Braut vor dem Brandenburger Tor – am Valentinstag (14. Februar 1990).

Wie kommt man nach Deutschland?

Wie wär's mit der Fähre?

Vergiß deine Reisetabletten nicht!

I've got my passport and I'm going to Germany tomorrow.

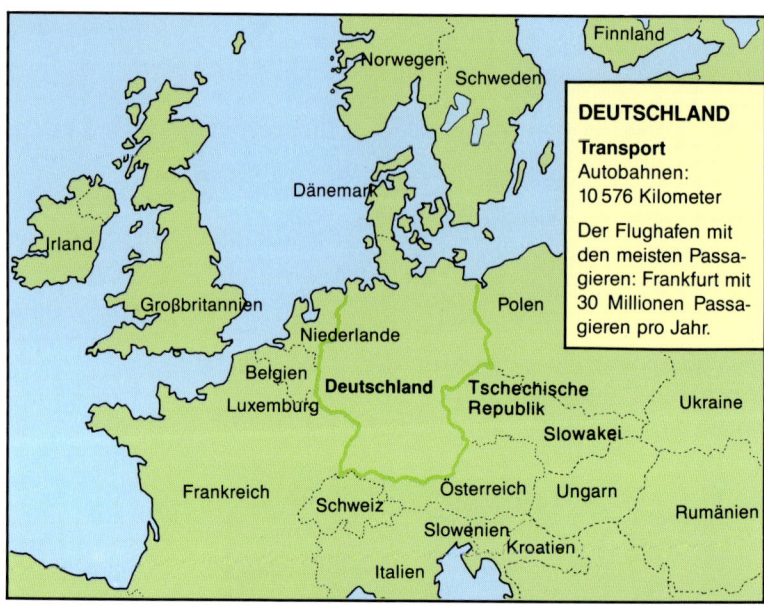

DEUTSCHLAND
Transport
Autobahnen:
10 576 Kilometer

Der Flughafen mit den meisten Passagieren: Frankfurt mit 30 Millionen Passagieren pro Jahr.

Germany is situated in the middle of Europe. It is linked to the countries surrounding it by extensive air, rail and road networks. Inside Germany, there are 10,576 km (6,567 miles) of motorways.

Frankfurt Airport, near the city of Frankfurt am Main, is the country's busiest airport. It is also one of Europe's main airports (after London and Paris) and a central hub in world air travel, because many people flying in from outside Europe change planes in Frankfurt. Approximately 29 million German and foreign passengers pass through Frankfurt Airport every year.

Germany's most important sea port, and one of Europe's main ports, is Hamburg on the **Nordsee** (North Sea) coast in the north of the country. Passenger ferries operate from Hamburg across the **Nordsee** to Britain. Visitors from Sweden, Norway, Denmark and Finland cross the **Ostsee** (Baltic Sea) by ferry to ports on Germany's Baltic coast.

1. Look at the map. If you are visiting Germany, which method of transport do you think you would use for the following journeys? Explain why.
   a) Going from Belgium to the north west of Germany.
   b) Going from Austria to the centre of Germany.
   c) Going from Britain to the north of Germany.

Man kann auch fliegen

Look at the photo. The plane belongs to the German airline, Lufthansa. Near which airport was the photo taken?

On a map, find all the towns marked on the road signs.

Das Fliegen ist so schön – keine Staus, keine Abgase!

Über den Rhein!

Wenn du mit dem Auto oder mit dem Zug fährst, wirst du wahrscheinlich über unseren größten und berühmtesten Fluß, den Rhein, fahren.

Das Bundeshaus in Bonn

Die Pfalz – ein altes Zollamt am Rhein

The Rhine's source is in Switzerland, and 1,320 km later (876 of them in Germany) it flows into the North Sea at Rotterdam, in the Netherlands.

It is of major economic importance to Germany as it provides a transportation link between the South, the industrial Ruhr area and the North Sea.

The castles, picturesque towns and vineyards of the Middle Rhine between Bonn and Bingen attract many tourists. The **Bundeshaus** (German Parliament) is on the banks of the Rhine, in Bonn.

One of the many legends about the Rhine concerns a beautiful girl named Loreley who sang so sweetly high above the river on a rock (which was named after her) that the sailors below forgot about navigating, and were shipwrecked and drowned. Nowadays the music sounds a little different, since the **Loreley** is famous for the Open Air Rock Festivals held there every year.

Übung macht den Meister

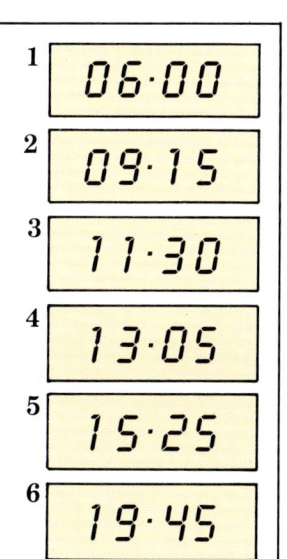

You may have to put your watch forward an hour when you reach the Continent. You can check on the boat or the plane. Make sure you understand the 24-hour clock. It is used a great deal in Germany.

Practise telling the time. Start with the clocks on the right, then try the 24-hour times on the left.

Wie spät ist es?
Wieviel Uhr ist es?

If you want to know the time, you can use either of these questions.

Was soll ich mitnehmen?

Ohne Geld kommt man nicht weit

Nimmst du Bargeld oder Reiseschecks mit?

You can buy your currency for the German-speaking countries – **D-Mark** for Germany, **Schillinge** for Austria and **Franken** for Switzerland – at home before you leave, on the ferry or at the airport, or in the country after you have arrived. You may want to take **Reiseschecks** (traveller's cheques) with you. These will be refunded if lost or stolen, but must be ordered in advance.

When you need a bank, look for the signs shown here or ask people: „**Wo ist die nächste Bank?**".

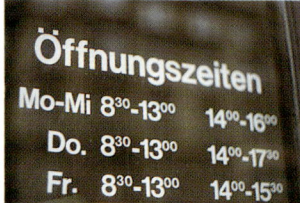

1 Wann macht die Bank links auf?
2 An welchem Tag hat sie länger auf?
3 Hat sie samstags geöffnet?
4 Wie lange hat sie mittags zu?
5 Hat die Bank länger geöffnet als die Banken in England?

Deutsche Banknoten und Münzen. Wie viele Pfennige hat eine Mark?

Österreichische Schillinge und Groschen. Wie viele Groschen sind in einem Schilling?

Schweizer Franken und Rappen. Wie viele Rappen hat ein Franken?

Übung macht den Meister

You are on holiday in Germany and you go into a German bank. How would you ask to change:
1 £10?
2 £20?
3 £15 in traveller's cheques?
4 £25 in traveller's cheques?

Look in a newspaper to find out what the exchange rate is today.

Bloß nicht so viel Gepäck!

Here's my luggage list. I hope I haven't forgotten anything!

Daniel is off to Germany on holiday now. Match the correct name to each numbered object, then compile a list in German of things you think he has forgotten.

Remember: If you haven't got a British passport, check with the embassies of the countries you are travelling to (and through). You may need a visa. If you are going to Germany, get a form E111 from your local Social Security office or post office. This form tells you how to get free medical treatment in EC countries.

```
Paß              Geld/Reiseschecks
Hemden           Versicherung
Pulli            Fotoapparat
Schuhe           Unterwäsche
Anorak           Kuli/Schreibpapier
Jeans/Hose       Adreßbuch
Notizbuch        Wörterbuch
Socken           Toilettenartikel
                 Sonnenbrille
```

Nützliche Ausdrücke

Here are a few expressions you might find useful in Germany. Can you link them to the correct English expressions?

1. (Guten) Tag.
2. (Auf) Wiedersehen.
3. Tschüs!
4. Wie geht's?
5. Mir geht's gut.
6. Ich habe (keinen) Hunger.
7. Ich habe (keinen) Durst.
8. Ich bin satt.
9. Ich bin müde.
10. Ich muß aufs Klo.

a) I'm fine.
b) How are you?
c) Goodbye.
d) I need a loo.
e) I'm (not) thirsty.
f) Hallo.
g) I'm tired.
h) I'm full up.
i) I'm (not) hungry.
j) Cheerio.

Wie wird das Wetter?

Lies diese Wettervorhersage aus einer deutschen Zeitung und beantworte diese Fragen:

1. Wie wird das Wetter heute:
   (a) in Norddeutschland?   (b) in Süddeutschland?
   (c) in der Schweiz?   (d) in Österreich?
2. In welchen Städten war es gestern in Europa am wärmsten?
3. In welchen Ländern sind die Städte auf der Liste rechts? Schreibe ihre Namen auf deutsch auf!

Was mußt du noch mitnehmen, wenn du zum Skilaufen fährst?

Es gibt so viel zu sehen!

Wissenswertes über deutschsprachige Länder

Ich verreise oft und gern. Fotografieren ist mein Hobby. Hier sind einige Fotos aus meinem Album.

Eine Wattwanderung zwischen zwei friesischen Inseln macht viel Spaß!

Ich komme aus Dortmund. Hier sehen Sie den Westfalenpark und das Stahlwerk Hoesch.

Länder und Kantone

There are 16 **Länder** (federal states) in Germany and nine in Austria. The **Länder** are shown on the map below in italics. (See page 5.)

In Switzerland the regions are called **Kantone**. About 75 per cent of Swiss people speak **Schwyzerdütsch** (Swiss German). Do you know what other languages are spoken in Switzerland?

Die Sommerferien

To prevent too much chaos on the roads, the **Länder** in the old West Germany stagger the dates of their school holidays. Look at the dates for the summer holidays for the years 1992-94 and answer these questions in German:

1 An welchem Tag fangen die Sommerferien 1992 in Berlin an?
2 In welchem Land fangen die Sommerferien 1993 am ersten Juli an?
3 Wo fangen die Ferien 1994 am frühesten an?
4 Welche Länder haben im September 1994 noch Ferien?

Langfristige Sommerferienregelung 1992 bis 1994

Land	1992	1993	1994
Baden-Württ.	2.7.–15.8.	1.7.–14.8.	7.7.–20.8.
Bayern	30.7.–14.9.	22.7.– 6.9.	28.7.–12.9.
Berlin	25.6.– 8.8.	24.6.– 7.8.	21.7.– 3.9.
Bremen	25.6.– 8.8.	18.6.–31.7.	21.7.– 3.9.
Hamburg	18.6.– 1.8.	5.7.–14.8.	18.7.–27.8.
Hessen	18.6.– 1.8.	29.7.–13.9.	14.7.–24.8.
Niedersachsen	25.6.– 5.8.	18.6.–31.7.	21.7.–31.8.
Nordrhein-Westf.	16.7.–29.8.	8.7.–21.8.	23.6.– 6.8.
Rheinland-Pfalz	23.7.– 2.9.	15.7.–25.8.	30.6.–10.8.
Saarland	23.7.– 5.9.	15.7.–28.8.	30.6.–13.8.
Schleswig-Holst.	18.6.– 1.8.	2.7.–14.8.	14.7.–27.8.

Das idyllische Dorf Schönbach in Österreich.

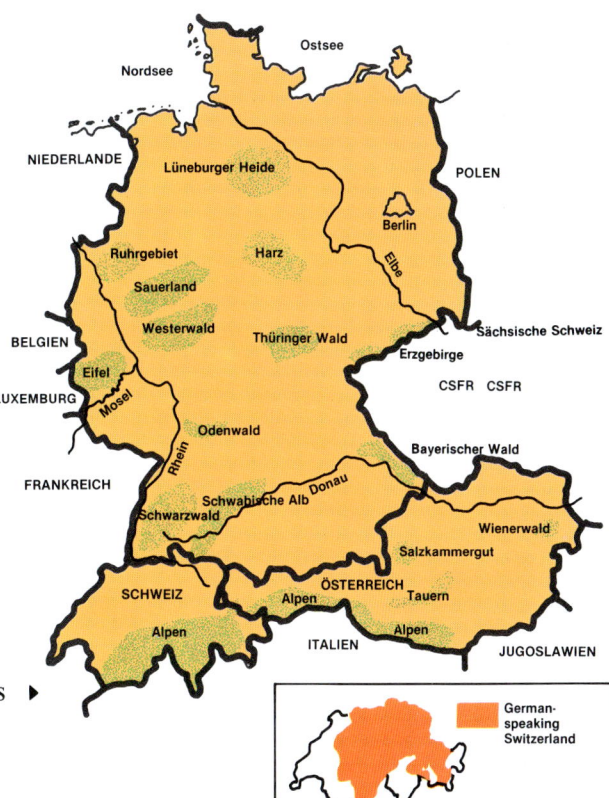

The scenery in German-speaking Europe is varied and often very beautiful. This map shows the main geographical features.

Wer spricht deutsch?

Look how many people speak German:

In Deutschland: 78 Millionen
In Österreich: 7 Millionen
In der Schweiz: 4 Millionen
In Liechtenstein: 18 Tausend

Even some people in Luxembourg, France and Italy speak it. But though the written language is the same, the dialects in the spoken language are so strong that a North German finds it difficult to understand a Bavarian, an Austrian, or a Swiss speaking **Schwyzerdütsch**. Sometimes even the words are different. Look at this list of North German and Austrian differences (some of the Austrian words are heard in South Germany too).

Norddeutschland	*Österreich*
Guten Tag!	Grüß Gott!
Auf Wiedersehen!	Auf Wiederschauen!
Junge	Bub
Treppe	Stiege
Januar	Jänner
dieses Jahr	heuer
zu Hause	daheim
gucken	schauen

Don't worry – most people will speak standard German **Hochdeutsch** with you! But it's fun to try and spot local dialects and words when you can.

Wir wollen mehr herausfinden

If you are going to Germany, your local travel agent may be able to give you some leaflets about the place you are going to. Or you could drop a line to the **Verkehrsamt** (Tourist Information Office) in the nearest big town to where you will be. Ask them to send you some information. Use this model letter.

> Cardiff, den 4. März
>
> Sehr geehrte Damen und Herren,
>
> In sechs Wochen fahren wir mit unserer Klasse nach Wiesbaden. Wir würden uns sehr freuen, wenn Sie uns einige Prospekte über Wiesbaden und Umgebung zusenden könnten.
>
> Wir danken Ihnen im voraus für Ihre Mühe.
>
> Mit freundlichen Grüßen,
> Andy Sparrow

Zwei Hauptstädte

Bonn

Große Überraschung

It was a great surprise to many when, on November 3, 1949, Bonn was chosen as a "temporary" federal capital for West Germany. Until that time, the 2000-year-old city, a third of which was destroyed during World War II, was known as a Roman settlement, residence of the **Kölner Kurfürsten** (Electors of Cologne), traditional university town and birthplace of the composer Beethoven. Who would have thought that for the next 42 years a small provincial town like Bonn would play such an important role on the world stage?

Die frühere Residenz der Kölner Kurfürsten ist heute die Universität Bonn.

Das Haus, in dem Beethoven 1770 geboren wurde.

Große Enttäuschung

So the disappointment was that much greater when, on June 20, 1991, the German parliament voted Berlin as the new seat of government for a reunited Germany.

The vote was a close one (338 for Berlin, 320 for Bonn), and it may be many years before Berlin is in a position to take back its former role as capital. In Bonn, the end of an era had come, despite demonstrations (see the photo on the right) to protest the vote.

Der heutige Stadtkern

Political activity in Bonn's present-day city takes place around the **Bundeshaus** (Germany's federal parliament building) and the offices for the administration and the parliamentary representatives. The buildings stand on the bank of the Rhine (see page 13).

Everyday life in the city, however, centers around the quaint **Marktplatz** (marketplace) with its Gothic city hall, around the **Münsterplatz** with its 900-year-old **Münsterkirche** (cathedral church) and the traffic-free zone between the two squares.

Der Marktplatz und das Rathaus (rechts). Der Markt findet an jedem Werktag statt.

Berlin

Freude – aber Probleme

In 1871, Berlin became the capital of the newly united German state. It has now been again named capital of the reunited Germany; something that might have been hard to imagine before the events of November 1989. Who could forget the feeling of **Freude** (joy) when on November 9 the Berlin Wall was opened up?

West Berlin had lived through an unusual post-war experience: its isolated position in the middle of the GDR gave the city a special status. In 1948, the city was kept going during the year-long Soviet blockade by a massive airlift of food and other supplies (see page 8). Later, low tax rates and a high level of state subsidy from the government in Bonn helped the city to develop.

For three decades the western half of the city was closed off by walls and barbed wire. It was cut off from the GDR's showcase city, East Berlin which, like West Berlin, was supported by state subsidies. There is now great joy in Berlin, but there are also new difficulties to face.

Die ersten Schwierigkeiten

The problems are increasing because the people living in the eastern part of the city want to work in the western side where they can earn twice as much. At the moment the German state cannot afford to bring ex-GDR salaries up to the same level as the ex-West German ones.

A lot of building has to be done before politicians and diplomats can move to Berlin. And it will be some time until East and West Berliners, who have such very different experiences of the recent past, can come closer to each other.

Das Brandenburger Tor war früher ein Symbol der Teilung Deutschlands. Heute symbolisiert es die Einheit der Nation.

Die Zukunft

Looking to the future – what might Berlin look like in ten years? With its variety of cultures and languages it will certainly develop into a lively, colorful and economically powerful city – a great contrast to the quiet, cozy former capital on the banks of the Rhine.

Der Berliner Bär ist das Symbol Berlins. Man sieht den Bär an Bussen, Zügen und Müllwagen in Berlin. ▶

Das alte Olympiastadion ▶

Einige Städte

Deutschlands Stadt-Hitparade

Stadt	Einwohner
1 Berlin	3 400 000
2 Hamburg	1 585 900
3 München	1 266 100
4 Köln	919 300
5 Essen	622 000
6 Frankfurt am Main	598 000
7 Dortmund	575 200
8 Düsseldorf	563 000
9 Stuttgart	561 200
10 Leipzig	550 000

Finde diese 10 Städte auf einer Landkarte.

1 Wie viele sind in Süddeutschland?
2 Wie viele sind im Ruhrgebiet?
3 Wie viele sind in der ehemaligen DDR?
4 Welche Flüsse fließen durch diese Städte?
5 Wie viele Einwohner hat die Stadt, in der du wohnst? Ordne sie in die Liste ein!

Sechs berühmte Städte

Hamburg

Hamburg is probably more famous for its water than for its land! It is the most important port in Germany, with thousands of ships arriving and departing every year. Hamburg is also Germany's second largest industrial city (after Berlin), and an important printing town, with 4·5 million newspapers being produced there every day. It also has a famous football team – the **HSV (Hamburger Sportverein)**.

Dresden

Dresden is another beautiful city. It is situated on the river Elbe in the Eastern part of Germany (formerly the GDR). Dresden was heavily bombed at the end of World War II and has been painstakingly rebuilt. Its most famous building is the **Zwinger**, a palace which also had to be restored after 1945, and which houses many fine collections of art and china.

Zürich

Zürich is the largest city in Switzerland and is the centre of Swiss banking. Beautifully situated among the Swiss Alps, on the shores of Lake Zürich, the city is also a popular tourist centre. James Joyce, the Irish writer, said of Zürich: "Zürich is so clean that, should you spill your soup on the **Bahnhofstraße**, you could eat it up without a spoon."

Ein Blick auf Zürich, den See und die Berge

◀ *Der Hafen ist das Herz Hamburgs.*

Der Zwinger in Dresden

Das Olympia-Stadion in München wurde für die Olympischen Spiele 1972 gebaut.

München
Munich is one of the most beautiful cities in Germany. It is the capital of **Bayern** (Bavaria), an important agricultural area which extends down to the German Alps. The Bavarians consider themselves apart from the rest of Germany, especially from the "Prussian" North and East. They even have their own border signs (right).

Wien
The capital of Austria, Vienna is a city of music, theatre, good food, beautiful parks and the world-famous Spanish Riding School. It also holds many treasures of the Habsburgs, the old rulers of the Austro-Hungarian Empire.

Salzburg
Salzburg, just across the Austrian border from Germany, is a lovely city dominated by the **Festung** (castle). Since 1920 Salzburg has become world famous for its **Festspiele**, a summer festival of drama and music.

Die Pferde der Spanischen Reitschule heißen „Lipizzaner."

Die Festung und das Festspielhaus (rechts im Bild) in Salzburg.

Ein Städte-Quiz

Fill in the blanks in the following paragraph, using the names from the list below.

Frankfurt   Berlin
Bonn   Wien
Bern   Genf   München

Im Jahre 1936 fanden die Olympischen Spiele in __(a)__ statt, 36 Jahre später in __(b)__ . Das Finanzzentrum von Deutschland ist __(c)__, aber die Regierung befindet sich im Moment noch in __(d)__ .

Der Sitz des roten Kreuzes ist in __(e)__ in der Schweiz, obwohl die Hauptstadt __(f)__ ist. __(g)__ in Österreich is für seinen Knabenchor bekannt.

Hinaus in die Natur

„Mein Vater war ein Wandersmann"

This is the first line of a famous German song. Do you know what it is called in English?

The Germans have plenty of varied and beautiful countryside and they enjoy it to the full for **Wandern**, **Radfahren**, **Skilaufen** and **Rodeln**. What are these called in English?

Many areas have boards showing routes for **Wanderwege** (country hikes). These tell you how long a walk takes and which signs you should follow.

Ein Wegweiser in Freudenberg. Nach 200 Metern kann man dieses tolle Foto von einer der schönsten deutschen Städte machen.

Wanderwege in Dortmund

Look at the board above, showing walks near Dortmund, and answer these questions in German.

1 Wie lange dauert die Wanderung nach Herdecke?
2 Wo beginnt die Wanderung nach Witten?
3 Welche Wanderung ist am kürzesten?
4 Welchem Schild muß ich folgen, wenn ich zum Tierpark gehen möchte?

Eine Winterlandschaft

Das macht Spaß!

Weg gesperrt – Kennwort, bitte!

A

B

C

It's great fun to be out in the snow – but of course snow and ice bring their own dangers.

What do you think these signs mean?

Wie wär's mit einem Glas Wein?

Meine Eltern meinen, daß deutscher Wein der allerbeste ist. Ich darf auch ab und zu mal ein Glas trinken!

Although Germany has only 1% of the world's wine-producing area, its wines are famous all over the world. Particularly well-known are wines from the **Rhein** (sold in brown bottles) and the **Mosel** (sold in green bottles). **Franken** wines are sold in distinctive flask-shaped bottles known as **Bocksbeutel**.

Austria also produces fine wines, mainly in the east of the country, south of Vienna.

*This wine bar has an unusual name, it's called the **Wein-Sanatorium**.*

Eine kleine Auswahl an Weinsorten in einem deutschen Supermarkt. Die Weine sind nach Gebieten gruppiert.

Etiketten von Weinflaschen

The labels on wine bottles tell you the quality of the wine inside. The wines range (in quality and price) from **Tafelwein** to **Qualitätswein**, **Kabinett**, **Spätlese**, **Auslese** and **Eiswein**. The later the grapes are picked, the sweeter the wine will be. The grapes for an **Eiswein** should be just touched by frost before they are picked. In some areas, this may be as late as the New Year.

From which area and of what quality is each of the two wines on the right?

Die wichtigsten Weingebiete Deutschlands

1. Ahr
2. Mittelrhein
3. Mosel-Saar-Ruwer
4. Nahe
5. Rheingau
6. Rheinhessen
7. Hessische Bergstraße
8. Franken
9. Rheinpfalz
10. Württemberg
11. Baden

In den Bergen

If you go to the mountains, you will probably have the chance to travel by **Seilbahn** (cable car) or by **Sesselbahn** (chair-lift) like these two boys on a trip from their London school.

Wir treffen euch wieder unten!

Im Hotel

Wo kann man übernachten?

Die Hotels sind nicht so teuer bei uns!

If you need a room for the night, look out for signs like the ones in these photos. The better the facilities, the more you have to pay.

The symbols below are taken from a hotel guide. Which symbol goes with which explanation?

1  2  3  4 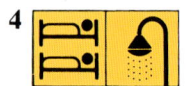 5  6   7

A Doppelzimmer ohne Bad/Dusche **B** Doppelzimmer mit Dusche

C Einzelzimmer mit Bad **D** Restaurant **E** Lift **F** Parkplatz **G** Zimmertelefon

Was kostet die Übernachtung?

Study this price list from a hotel in Oberursel, a town north of Frankfurt, and answer the questions in German.

1. Was ist die Postleitzahl von Oberursel?
2. Was ist die Vorwahl für Oberursel?
3. Sind diese Preise mit Bedienung und Mehrwertsteuer?
4. Zu welcher Zeit ist Hochsaison?
5. Was kostet das billigste Einzelzimmer?
6. Was kostet das teuerste Doppelzimmer?
7. Wieviel kostet ein Extra-Bett?
8. Stell dir vor, du übernachtest mit deinen Eltern in diesem Hotel. Ihr nehmt das billigste Doppelzimmer mit einem Extra-Bett. Wieviel müßt ihr zahlen?
9. Welche Abfahrt muß man nehmen, wenn man von der Autobahn kommt?
10. Wo muß man aussteigen, wenn man mit der Straßenbahn fährt?

Was kann man hier unternehmen?

If you're staying in the same hotel for a few days or more, you'll probably want to find out what there is to see and do in the area. Many hotels have some brochures and other information available at the reception desk.

Wenn du in diesem Hotel in Andernach übernachtest, kannst du die Burg Katz am Rhein besuchen (rechts).

Übung macht den Meister

Ich hoffe, daß dein Hotel gemütlicher ist als dieses hier in Burghausen!

Dieses Hotel heißt „Vier Jahreszeiten". Wie heißen die vier Jahreszeiten auf Deutsch?

You have just arrived at a hotel in Germany. How would you ask at the reception desk:
1 if they have a single room with a shower and toilet?
2 what the room costs?
3 whether this includes breakfast?
4 on what floor the room is?
5 if the room has a TV set?

Wo kann ich billig übernachten?

In der Jugendherberge

Es macht Spaß, in einer Jugendherberge zu übernachten. Man lernt so viele neue Leute kennen!

Tischtennis vor der Jugendherberge in Bayreuth

Germany has about 700 **Jugendherbergen** (youth hostels), Austria has 129 and Switzerland 89. People from many countries stay there, as they provide a cheap and friendly way of travelling. In addition to **Schlafsäle** (dormitories), many youth hostels have **Familienzimmer** (rooms for families), too. Meals can be taken in most hostels and in some you can cook for yourself. If you're going to stay in a youth hostel, don't forget your **Mitgliedsausweis** (membership card).

Die älteste Jugendherberge der Welt in einer alten Burg in Altena

Was kann man dort machen?

Look at this extract from the **Jugendherbergsverzeichnis** (Youth Hostel Handbook) for the Bayreuth hostel in the photo above.

Jugendherberge Bayreuth
Lage des Hauses: Bayreuth ist eine junge Universitätsstadt mit 70000 Einwohnern. Die JH grenzt unmittelbar an das städt. Freibad. Bis zur Stadtmitte ca. 15 Min. Gehweg.
Anreise (Bahnn, Linienbus): Nürnberg–Bayreuth, Buslinie Birken.
Anreise (Reisebus, PKW): BAB A 9 Nürnberg–Berlin, Ausfahrt Bayreuth Süd.
Besonders geeignet für: Schullandheimaufenthalte, Sportgruppen, Erholungsfreizeiten, Tagungen, Familien.
Freizeitangebote: Freiluftschach, Fußball-, Federball- und Volleyballplatz, Disco, Kegelbahn und Grillplatz. In der Stadt: Hallen- und Freibad, Eislaufbahn, reizvolle Parkanlagen.
Besichtigungen: Festspielhaus und historische Sammlungen. Die abwechslungsreiche Landschaft in der Umgebung bietet auf guten Wegen viele Wandermöglichkeiten. Bus- und Stadtrundfahrten können organisiert werden.

1 What do we learn about Bayreuth?
2 What is next to the hostel?
3 How far from the town is the hostel?
4 What leisure facilities are available at the hostel?
5 What is there to do in the town?
6 What in particular does the countryside offer?
7 What can be organised?

Was bedeutet DJH?

Was kostet die Jugendherberge?

There are six categories of youth hostels, and prices for an overnight stay vary depending on the quality of the building, the facilities, and the popularity of the town or the area.

Look at the list of charges for youth hostels below and answer the questions in German.

Gebühren
Übernachtungsgebühr für Junioren
   (bis 26 Jahre) .... ca. DM 13,- bis 15,-
Leihgebühr für 1 Schlafsack (bis zu 10 Tagen)
   .... DM 2,- bis 3,-
Leihgebühr für 2 Bettlaken (bis zu 10 Tagen)
   .... DM 3,- bis 3,50
Für vollständige Bettwäsche bei Daueraufenthalten
   (1 Bettlaken, 1 Bettbezug, 1 Kopfkissen
   bis zu 10 Tagen) .... DM 4,- bis 6,-
Einzelmahlzeiten .... ca. DM 4,50 bis 8,-
Vollverpflegung .... ca. DM 13,50 bis 18,-

Was kostet es:
1 eine Nacht zu übernachten?
2 einen Schlafsack zu leihen?
3 die komplette Bettwäsche für eine Woche zu leihen?
4 das teuerste Mittagessen zu essen?
5 alle drei Mahlzeiten pro Tag in der Jugendherberge zu essen?

Auf dem Campingplatz

Wir zelten gern. An der frischen Luft schlafen wir immer gut.

Campsites are even cheaper to stay in than youth hostels and the facilities are usually very good. You just have to hope the weather is equally good!

Das Ruhrgebiet ist nicht überall grau und häßlich. Auf diesem Foto fließt die Ruhr am Campingplatz Hohensyburg vorbei.

Habe ich an alles gedacht?

1 Ich habe meinen Schlafsack mit.

2 Ich habe meine Luftmatratze ...

3 ... meinen Campingkocher.

4 Hier ist mein Geschirr

5 ... und mein Besteck.

6 Ach, nein – ich habe mein Zelt vergessen!

Was darf man auch nicht vergessen, wenn man einen Campingurlaub macht? Schreib eine Liste von Sachen, die du mitnehmen würdest.

Übung macht den Meister

You have just arrived at a youth hostel. How would you:
1 ask if they have any space?
2 say that you wish to stay three nights?
3 ask where the dormitories, wash-rooms and toilets are?
4 ask what time breakfast is?
5 ask if you can cook there?

Meike and her friend have just arrived at a campsite. How would they ask:
6 if there is space?
7 what it costs for a tent and two people for one night?
8 if there are a shop and a restaurant on the site?
9 where they should pitch their tent?
10 what there is to do in the area?

Haben Sie Ihre Ausweise dabei?

Ein deutsches Haus

Was ist anders?

Are the houses very different in Germany?

If you visit a German house, you will see a lot of everyday things that look a little different – doors, windows, plugs and sockets, for example.

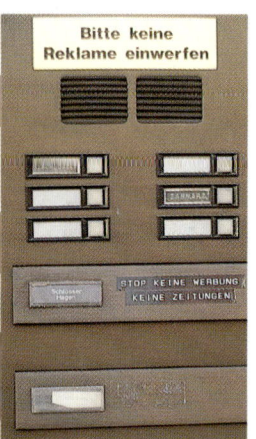 

Look at the windows and doors above. With the handles horizontal, this type of door and window is wide open. With the handles up, they open **auf Kipp** (leaning). With the handles down, they are **geschlossen** (shut).

Electric plugs in Germany are two-prong. The earth is a metal strip on the edge of the plug.

Many blocks of flats have letter boxes and an intercom system like the one on the far left. What is the request above the loudspeaker?

Shutters are very widely used in Germany. What do you think are their advantages? There are two different types: **Fensterläden** are shutters that open out and **Rolläden** are shutters that wind down.

Dieses Haus in Salzburg in Österreich hat Fensterläden.

Das Haus von Matthias hat Rolläden.

Der Keller macht so viel aus!

Houses in Germany are usually more spacious than they look because most have a cellar. Even apartments have a small store room in the basement of the building. This **Reihenhaus** (terraced house) in which Matthias lives has a large cellar. There are four rooms in it: **der Heizungskeller** (containing the heating equipment), **die Waschküche** (with a washing machine and tumble dryer), **ein Gästezimmer** (guest room) and **ein Vorratsraum** (storage room containing a freezer as well as bottled drinks, canned foods, fruit and vegetables).

Some of the contents of the storage room are shown in the photo below. Make a list of the things in German.

Wir haben auch eine Tischtennisplatte im Gästezimmer, und ab und zu feiern wir Parties im Keller.

Übung macht den Meister

Und hier ist unser Wohnzimmer.

If you were staying with a German family, how would you ask:
1 how long they have been living in their home?
2 if they like living there?
3 if they have relatives living nearby?
4 where they would most like to live?
5 what their dream house would be like?

Aber nicht zu viele Fragen stellen!

1 „Was essen Sie am liebsten?"
„Mein Lieblingsgericht ist Gulasch mit Nudeln."

2 „Trinken Sie gern Wein?"
„O ja, vor allem Moselwein."

3 „Wie oft gehen Sie abends aus?"
„Nur selten. Wir sind immer zu müde."

4 „Fahren Sie oft in Urlaub?"
„Einmal im Jahr — meistens nach Spanien oder Italien."

5 „Was machen Sie am liebsten in Ihrer Freizeit?"
„Ich koche und backe gern und höre gern Musik."

6 „Was machen Sie nicht so gern?"
„So viele Fragen beantworten!"

In einer deutschen Familie

Darf ich mich vorstellen?

If you're going on an exchange trip, it's a good idea to write a short letter to your exchange partner first – like this one. Send a photo, too!

> Bedford, den 8. April
>
> Liebe Bärbel!
> Ich bin Deine Austauschpartnerin und freue mich sehr auf die zwei Wochen bei Dir.
> Ich heiße Ros, bin 14 Jahre alt und wohne in einer Mietwohnung. Wo wohnst Du? Ich habe einen Bruder Gary, er ist zwei Jahre älter als ich.
> Was machst Du gern in Deiner Freizeit? Ich spiele gern Tennis, schwimme gern und höre gern Musik. Mein Lieblingssänger ist Prince.
> Schreib mir alles über Dich und Deine Familie.
> Schöne Grüße,
> Ros

Ich bin Marcus aus Köln. Ich freue mich sehr auf den Besuch meiner Austauschpartnerins.

Wo wohnen die Deutschen?

Since the Second World War, many new homes have been built and old ones renovated. Many Germans own their own home but it is also quite common to rent a house or flat. A third of the population lives in large towns, usually in flats.

Diese Wohnblocks in Deutschland haben einen großen Spielplatz.

Ein Bauernhaus im Schwarzwald. Das Haus und der Kuhstall sind im selben Gebäude.

Straßenschilder und Verkehrszeichen

Ein Schilder-Quiz

A

B

C

H

D

Have a look at these signs.
1 Which one means:
   a) police?
   b) diversion?
   c) motorway exit?
   d) bridge over a valley?
   e) motorway merger?
   f) black ice?
2 What are you asked to do if there is a traffic jam?
3 a) What are you asked to do at the motorway car park?
   b) Where is the next toilet?

G

F

E

Einige Tips

If you break down, the **ADAC (Allgemeiner Deutscher Automobilclub)** will help. If you belong to an affiliated organisation, such as the AA, and have a **Schutzbrief** (5-star-insurance), there is no charge for calling out the **ADAC**. When you drive in Germany, you must have your **Führerschein, Kraftfahrzeugschein, Erste-Hilfe-Kasten and Warndreieck** with you in your car all the time. What do you think these are?

All German cars must be taken regularly to the **TÜV (Technischer Überwachungsverein)** for a mechanical check. They also need an **ASU (Abgassonderuntersuchung)**, an exhaust emission check.

In the mountains, **Schneeketten** and **Winterreifen** are an important part of a driver's equipment. What are they and why are they used?

Auf der Autobahn

The first **Autobahnen** (motorways) in Germany were built in 1928. (Do you know when the first ones were built where you live?) The network of German motorways was greatly extended in the Thirties and, of course, after World War II. Today you can travel right across German-speaking Europe by motorway.

The sign on the left welcomes you when you cross the border into Germany. It gives the compulsory and recommended speed limits. Which do you think is which? How do the German speed limits compare with the ones on motorways where you live?

Make sure you can change kilometres into miles! Remember, 8 km = 5 miles. So to get miles, divide the number of kilometres by 8 and multiply by 5.

Wie viele Meilen sind:
a) 16 km?   c) 100 km?
b) 50 km?   d) 130 km?

Ortseingang und Ortsausgang

When you arrive at a town, you see a sign giving the name of the town. The speed limit immediately becomes 50 km/hr. When you leave a town, you pass a sign with the name crossed out. This means you can increase your speed again.

Have you heard of Colditz? It is between Leipzig and Chemnitz, in the former GDR. Its castle, which you can see in the picture below, was used as a top security prison during World War II and there were many exciting attempts to escape.

Am Ortseingang...   *...am Ortsausgang.*

OG	Offenburg	SAD	Schwandorf	TÜ	Tübingen	
OH	Ostholstein/Eutin	SAW	Salzwedel	TUT	Tuttlingen	
OHA	Osterode	SB	Saarbrücken			
OHZ	Osterholz-Scharmbeck	SBG	Strasburg	UE	Uelzen	
		SBK	Schönebeck	UEM	Ueckermunde	
OL	Oldenburg	SC	Schwabach	UL	Ulm	
OR	Oranienburg	SCZ	Schleiz	UN	Unna	
OS	Osnabrück	SDH	Sondershausen			
OVL	Obervogtland	SDL	Stendal	VB	Vogelsberg Kreis	
OZ	Oschatz	SDT	Schwedt/Oder	VEC	Vechta	
		SE	Bad Segeberg	VER	Verden/Aller	
P	Potsdam	SEB	Sebnitz	VIE	Viersen	
PA	Passau	SEE	Seelow	VK	Völklingen	
PAF	Pfaffenhofen a.d. Ilm	SFA	Soltau/Fallingbostel	VS	Willingen/Schwenningen	
PAN	Pfarrkirchen/Rottal-Inn	SFB	Senftenberg			
		SFT	Staßfurt	W	Wuppertal	
PB	Paderborn	SG	Solingen	WAF	Warendorf	
PCH	Parchim	SGH	Sangershausen	WB	Wittenberg	
PE	Peine	SHA	Schwäbisch Hall	WBS	Worbis	
PER	Perleberg	SHG	Stadthagen	WDA	Werdau	
PF	Pforzheim	SHL	Suhl	WE	Weimar	
PI	Pinneberg	SI	Siegen	WEN	Weiden i.d. Opf.	
PIR	Pirna	SIG	Sigmaringen	WES	Wesel	
PK	Pritzwalk	SIM	Simmern	WF	Wolfenbüttel	
PL	Plauen	SK	Saalkreis/Halle	WHV	Wilhelmshaven	
PLÖ	Plön	SL	Schleswing/Flensburg	WI	Wiesbaden	
PN	Pößneck	SLF	Saalfeld	WIL	Bernkastell/Wittlich	
PS	Pirmasens	SLN	Schmölln	WIS	Wismar. Kreis	
PW	Pasewalk	SLS	Saarlouis	WK	Wittstock	
PZ	Prenzlau	SLZ	Bod Salzungen	WL	Winsen/Luhe	
QFT	Querfurt	SM	Schmalkalden	WLG	Wolgast	
QLB	Quedlinburg	SN	Schwerin	WM	Weilheim/Schongau	
		SON	SoestSonneberg	WMS	Wolmirstedt	
R	Regensburg	SOM	Sömmerda	WN	Waibingen	
RA	Rastatt	SP	Speyer	WND	St. Wendel	
RC	Reichenbach	SPB	Spremberg	WO	Worms	
RD	Rendsburg/Eckernförde	SR	Straubing/Bogen	WOB	Wolfsburg	
				WR	Wernigerode	
RDG	Ribnitz-Damgarten	SRB	Strausberg	WRN	Waren	
RE	Reckling-hausen	SRO	Stadtroda	WSF	Weißenfels	
REG	Regen	ST	Steinfurt	WST	Westerstede	
RH	Roth	STA	Starmberg	WSW	Weißwasser	
RIE	Riesa	STB	Sternberg	WT	Waldshut	
RL	Rochlitz	STD	Stade	WTM	Wittmund	
RM	Röbel/Müritz	STL	Stollberg	W1U	Würzburg	
RN	Rathenow	SU	Siegburg	WUG	Weißenburg/Gunzen hausen	
RO	Rosenheim	SÜW	Südliche Weinstraße			
ROS	Rostock Kreis			WUN	Wunsiedel	
ROW	Rotenburg/Wümme	SW	Schweinfurt	WUR	Wurzen	
		SZ	Salzgitter	WW	Westerwald	
RS	Remscheid	SZB	Schwarzenberg	WZL	Wanzleben	
RSL	Roßlau					
RT	Reutlingen	TBB	Tauberbischofsheim	Z	Zwickau	
RU	Rudolstadt	TET	Teterow	ZE	Zerbst	
RÜD	Rüdesheim	TG	Torgau	ZI	Zittau	
RUG	Rgen	TIR	Tirschenreuth	ZP	Zschopau	
RV	Ravensburg	TÖL	Bad Tölz/Wofrats-hausen	ZR	Zeulenroda	
RW	Rottweil			ZS	Zossen	
RZ	Ratzeburg	TP	Templin	ZW	Zweibrücken	
		TR	Trier	ZZ	Zeitz	
S	Stuttgart	TS	Traunstein			

Die Burg in Colditz. Wozu wird sie heute genutzt?

Auf der Straße

Woher kommt das Auto?

*Was für ein Auto bin ich?
Aus welcher Stadt komme ich?*

Here are the symbols of five other makes of German cars. Can you link the correct name to each symbol?

In Germany it is easy to work out where a car comes from. Just look at the first letter(s) of the registration plate and consult the chart below. You may see some other registrations but they are gradually being phased out.

The letters **HH**, on the cartoon car's registration, stand for **Hansestadt Hamburg**. The **Hansestädte** were a group of North German trading towns who combined in the Middle Ages to protect their interests overseas (and fought trade wars with Denmark and England).

**Mercedes   Opel   Audi
BMW   Volkswagen**

In Austria, cars have the first letter(s) of their **Bundesland** (see page 16). For example, W=**Wien**, St=**Steiermark**.

Deutsche Kraftfahrzeug-Kennzeichen ab 1. Januar 1991

ADAC

A	Augsburg	BZ	Bautsen	ESA	Eisenach	GVM	Grevesmühlen	JE	Jessen	ME	Mettmann
AA	Aalen			ESW	Eschwege	GW	Greifswald, Kr.			MEI	Meißen
AB	Aschaffenburg	C	Chemnitz	EU	Euskirchen	GZ	Günzburg	K	Köln	MER	Merseburg
ABG	Altenburg	CA	Calau	EW	Eberswalde			KA	Karlsruhe	MG	Mönchengladbach
AC	Aachen	CB	Cottbus			H	Hannover	KB	Korbach	MGN	Meiningen
AE	Auerbach	CE	Celle	F	Frankfurt/M.	HA	Hagen	KC	Kronach	MH	Mülheim a.d. Ruhr
AIC	Aichach	CHA	Cham	FB	Friedberg	HAL	Halle	KE	Kempten	MHL	Mühlhausen
AK	Altenkirchen	CLP	Cloppenburg	FD	Fulda	HAM	Hamm	KEH	Kelheim	MI	Minden/Lübbecke
AM	Amberg/Opf.	CO	Coburg	FDS	Freudenstadt	HAS	Hassfurth	KF	Kaufbeuren	MIL	Miltenberg
AN	Ansbach	COC	Cochem	FF	Frankfurt/O.	HB	Bremen	KG	Bad Kissingen	MK	Märkischer Kreis
ANA	Annaberg	COE	Coesfeld	FFB	Fürstenfeldbruck	HBN	Hildburghausen	KH	Bad Kreuznach	MM	Memmingen
ANG	Angermünde	CUX	Cuxhaven	FG	Freiberg	HBS	Halberstadt	KI	Kiel	MN	Mindelheim
ANK	Anklam	CW	Calw	FI	Finsterwaide	HC	Hainichen	KIB	Kirchheim-Bolanden	MOS	Mosbach
AÖ	Altötting			FL	Fiensburg	HD	Heidelberg			MR	Marburg/Biedenkopf
APO	Apolda	D	Düsseldorf	FLÖ	Flöha	HDH	Heidenheim	KL	Kaiserslautern		
ARN	Arnstadt	DA	Darmstadt	FN	Friedrichshafen	HDL	Haldensleben	KLE	Kleve	MS	Münster
ART	Artern	DAH	Dachau	FO	Forchheim	HE	Helmstedt	KLZ	Klötze	MSP	Main/Spessart
AS	Amberg/Sulzbach	DAN	Lüchow/Dannenberg	FOR	Forst	HEF	Hersfeld/Rotenburg	KM	Kamenz	MTK	Main/Taunus-Kreis
ASL	Aschersleben			FR	Freiburg			KN	Konstanz	MÜ	Mühldorf a. Inn
AT	Altentreptow	DAU	Daun	FRG	Freyung/Grafenau	HEI	Heide	KO	Koblenz	MYK	Mayen/Koblenz
AU	Aue	DBR	Bad Doberan	FRI	Friesland	HER	Herne	KÖT	Köthen	MZ	Mainz
AUR	Aurich	DD	Dresden	FRW	Bad Freienwaide	HET	Hettstedt	KR	Krefeld	MZG	Merzig/Wadern
AW	Ahrweiler	DE	Dessau	FS	Freising	HF	Herford	KS	Kassel		
AZ	Alzey	DEG	Deggendorf	FT	Frankenthal	HG	Bad Homburg	KT	Kitzingen	N	Nürnberg
		DEL	Delmenhorst	FTL	Freital	HGN	Hagenow	KU	Kuimback	NAU	Nauen
B	Berlin	DGF	Dingolfing/Landau	FÜ	Fürth	HGW	Hansestadt Greifswald	KÜN	Künzelsau	NB	Neubrandenburg
BA	Bamberg	DH	Diepholz	FW	Fürstenwalde			KUS	Kusel	ND	Neuburg/Schroben-Hausen
BAD	Baden-Baden	DL	Döbeln			HH	Hamburg	KW	Königs-Wusterhausen		
BB	Böblingen	DLG	Dillingen	G	Gera	HHM	Hohenmölsen			NDH	Nordhausen
BBG	Bernburg	DM	Demmin	GA	Gardelegen	HI	Hildesheim	KY	Kyritz	NE	Neuss
BC	Biberach a. d. Riß	DN	Düren	GAP	Garmisch-Partenkirchen	HIG	Heiligenstadt			NEA	Neustadt a.d. Aisch
		DO	Dortmund	GC	Glauchau	HL	Lübeck	L	Leipzig	NEB	Nebra
BED	Brand-Erbisdorf	DON	Donauwörth	GDB	Gadebusch	HM	Hameln/Pyrmont	LA	Landshut	NES	Bad Neustadt a.d. Saale
BEL	Belzig	DU	Duisburg	GE	Gelsenkirchen	HN	Heilbronn	LAU	Lauf a. d. Pegnitz		
BER	Bernau	DÜW	Bad Dürkheim	GER	Germersheim	HO	Hof	LB	Ludwigsburg	NEW	Neustadt a.d. Waldnaab
BGL	Berchtesgadener Land	DW	Dippoldiswalde	GF	Gifhorn	HOL	Holzminden	LBS	Lobenstein		
BI	Bielefeld	DZ	Delitzsch	GG	Groß-Gerau	HOM	Homburg	LBZ	Lübz	NF	Husum
BIR	Birkenfeld			GHA	Geithain	HOT	Hohenstein-Ernstthal	LC	Luckau	NH	Neuhaus
BIT	Bitburg	E	Essen	GHC	Gräfenhainichen			LD	Landau/Pfalz	NI	Nienburg
BIW	Bischofswerda	EB	Eilenburg	GI	Giessen	HP	Heppenheim	LDK	Lahb-Dill-Kreis	NK	Neunkirchen
BL	Balingen	EBE	Ebersberg	GL	Bergisch-Gladbach	HR	Homberg	LER	Leer	NM	Neumarkt i.d. Opt.
BM	Bergheim	ED	Erding	GM	Gummersbach	HRO	Hansestadt Rostock	LEV	Leverkusen	NMB	Naumburg
BN	Bonn	EF	Erfurt	GMN	Grimmen	HS	Heinsberg	LG	Lüneburg	NMS	Neumünster
BNA	Borna	EH	Eisenhüttenstadt	GNT	Genthin	HSK	Hochsauer-land-Kreis	LI	Lindau	NOH	Nordhorn/Bentheim
BO	Bochum	EI	Eichstätt	GO	Güstrow			LIB	Bad Liebenwerda		
BOR	Borken	EIL	Eisleben	GÖ	Göttingen	HST	Stralsund	LIF	Lichtenfels	NOM	Northeim
BOT	Bottrop	EIS	Eisenberg	GP	Göppingen	HU	Hanau	LIP	Lippe/Detmold	NP	Neuruppin
BRA	Brake	EL	Emsland	GR	Görlitz	HV	Havelberg	LL	Landsberg a. Lech	NR	Neuwied/Rhein
BRB	Brandenburg	EM	Emmendingen	GRH	Großhain	HWI	Hansestadt Wismar	LM	Limburg/Weilburg	NU	Neu-Uim
BRG	Burg	EMD	Emden	GRM	Grimma			LN	Lübben	NW	Neustadt a.d. Weinstraße
BS	Braunschweig	EMS	Bad Ems	GRS	Gransee	HX	Höxter	LÖ	Lörrach		
BSK	Beeskow	EN	Schwelm/Ennepe	GRZ	Greiz	HY	Hoyerswerda	LOB	Löbau	NY	Niesky
BT	Bayreuth	ER	Eriangen	GS	Goslar	HZ	Herzberg	LSZ	Bad Langensalza	NZ	Neustrelitz
BTF	Bitterfeld	ERB	Erbach/Odenwald	GT	Gütersloh			LU	Ludwigshafen		
BÜS	Büsingen	ERH	Erlangen/Höchstadt	GTH	Gotha	IGB	St. Ingbert	LUK	Luckenwalde	OA	Oberallgäu
BZ	Bützow	ES	Esslingen	GUB	Guben	IL	Ilmenau	LWL	Ludwigslust	OAL	Ostallgäu
				GÜ	Güstrow	IN	Ingolstadt			OB	Oberhausen
						IZ	Itzehoe/Steinburg	M	München	OBG	Osterburg
								MA	Mannheim	OC	Oschersleben
						J	Jena	MAB	Marienberg	OD	Bad Oldesloe
						JB	Jüterbog	MB	Miesbach	OE	Olpe
								MC	Malchin	OF	Offenbach a. Main
								MD	Maggeburg		

Herzlich willkommen!

Muß ich die ganze Zeit Hände schütteln?

Yes, there will be a lot of handshaking if you're staying with a German family – but not as much as there used to be. Today the atmosphere in most families is relaxed and people don't expect you to shake hands when you get up in the morning or go to bed in the evening.

Remember to call a child and close friends **du**, several children **ihr**, and an adult **Sie**.

Don't expect a hot breakfast. You might get **ein gekochtes Ei** (a boiled egg), but otherwise Germans eat **Brot** (bread) or **Brötchen** (rolls) with **Aufschnitt** (cold sliced meats), **Käse** (cheese), **Marmelade** (jam) and **Butter**. There may also be **Müsli**, **Joghurt** or **Quark** (curd cheese).

Before starting to eat, people will probably wish you **Guten Appetit** (enjoy your meal), and you reply **Danke, gleichfalls** (and you, too).

If you want to offer a **Gastgeschenk** (present brought by a guest) to your German host family, try to think of something typical from your country that they might enjoy. What kind of **Gastgeschenk** would you take to Germany?

Man soll die Feste feiern, wie sie fallen

„Man soll die Feste feiern, wie sie fallen" is a well-known German expression. What do you think it means? The Germans certainly love celebrating and take every opportunity to do so. Some of the traditional occasions are:

Ostern
Children look in the garden on **Ostersonntag** (Easter Sunday) for **Ostereier** (Easter eggs) which the **Osterhase** (Easter bunny) has brought. Even real eggs get painted and decorated.

Weihnachten
Most families don't put up their **Weihnachtsbaum** (Christmas tree) until **Heiligabend** (Christmas Eve). That evening they have their **Bescherung** (opening of presents). Each member of the family has a **Weihnachtsteller** (a plate full of nuts, fruit and chocolates). Dinner on Christmas Eve is traditionally **Karpfen** (carp) or **Aal** (eel), while on Christmas Day goose, turkey or rabbit are usually served. Many families go to church either on Christmas Eve or early on Christmas Day.

Silvester
On **Silvester** (New Year's Eve) bottles of **Sekt** (sparkling wine) are opened at midnight. Then everyone goes out on to the street or balcony to welcome the New Year in with a firework display.

◀ *Diese Kinder haben gerade ihre Ostereier gefunden.*

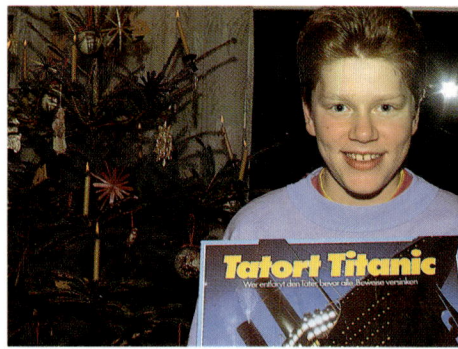

„Jetzt habe ich endlich das Spiel, das ich mir gewünscht habe!"

Willkommen im Neuen Jahr!

Wörter und Nummernschilder

Look at these German number plates. Which towns do the cars come from?

Can you form a German word out of the letters of each number plate and link it up to one of the definitions below?

1 eine Blume
2 etwas im Gesicht
3 ein Tier
4 etwas am Himmel
5 ein Behälter
6 jemand aus Großbritannien
7 etwas zu essen
8 wie man heißt
9 eine deutsche Stadt
10 Kurzform von „Johannes"

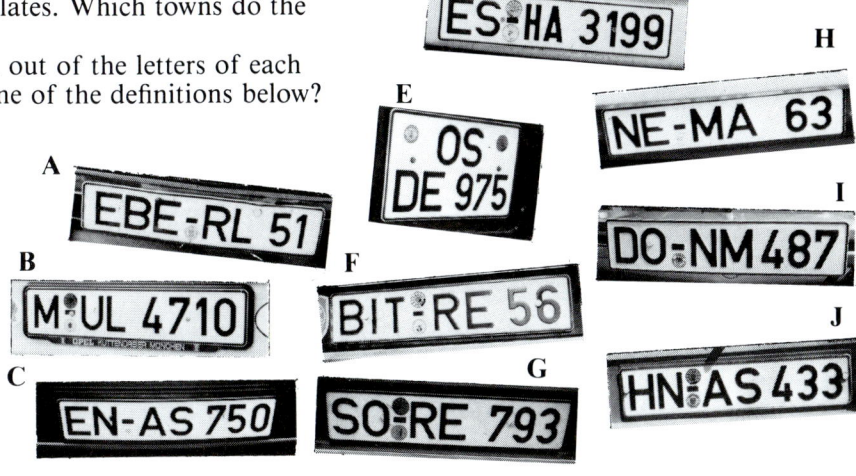

Übung macht den Meister

Wie weit ist es von München nach Wien?

Using the chart on the right, practise asking how far it is between any two cities.

Distances in kilometres	Aachen	Basel	Berlin	Bonn	Chemnitz	Dortmund	Dresden	Frankfurt	Hamburg	Köln	Leipzig	München	Salzburg	Stuttgart	Wien
Aachen		556	633	91	593	150	659	259	488	70	585	648	788	446	968
Basel	566		874	482	721	571	787	337	820	496	720	362	488	268	816
Berlin	633	874		598	271	488	205	555	289	569	179	584	724	624	805
Bonn	91	482	598		509	120	575	175	459	27	501	364	704	362	883
Chemnitz	593	721	271	509		541	76	403	483	515	80	418	558	458	773
Dortmund	150	571	488	120	541		607	264	343	83	532	653	793	451	1003
Dresden	659	787	205	575	76	607		469	502	589	108	484	624	524	853
Frankfurt	259	337	555	175	403	264	469		495	189	395	395	535	217	741
Hamburg	488	820	289	459	483	343	502	495		422	391	782	922	700	1122
Köln	70	496	569	27	515	83	589	189	422		515	578	718	376	907
Leipzig	585	720	179	501	80	532	108	395	391	515		425	565	465	739
München	648	362	584	364	418	653	484	395	782	578	425		138	220	419
Salzburg	788	488	724	704	558	793	624	535	922	718	565	138		360	282
Stuttgart	446	268	624	362	458	451	524	217	700	376	465	220	360		642
Wien	968	816	805	883	773	1003	853	741	1122	907	739	419	282	642	

Ein deutscher Witz

Wie heißt der chinesische Transportminister?

Um – lei – tung

An der Tankstelle

Auf der Autobahn

Ich muß unbedingt tanken!

Eine Autobahnraststätte

Most motorway service stations are named after the area in which they are to be found. The one on the right is in the **Wetterau**, a fertile plain to the north of Frankfurt am Main. In most service stations there is a whole range of facilities, for example **Toiletten**, **ein Café**, **ein Restaurant**, **ein Geschäft**, **ein Kinderspielplatz**, **Picknicktische**. Do you know what all these are?

Eine halbe Stunde Schaukeln ist so schön nach der langen Fahrt!

Diese Raststätte ist besonders schön gelegen – im Siegerland, zwischen Dortmund und Frankfurt.

Volltanken, bitte!

There are three grades of petrol available in Germany: **Normal** (usually just called **Benzin**), **Super** and **Super-Plus**. Germans are encouraged to buy lead-free petrol (**bleifrei**) rather than leaded (**verbleit**) and all new cars are manufactured to take it. **Normal/Benzin** can only be bought lead-free. All petrol is sold in litres.

Look at the photos of the Shell petrol prices and the petrol pump, and answer these questions in German:
1. Was kostet ein Liter Normal bei Shell?
2. Ist Super verbleit bei Shell teurer oder billiger als Super bleifrei?
3. Wie viele Liter Super hat man an der Zapfsäule gekauft?
4. Wieviel muß man an Zapfsäule 2 bezahlen?
5. Wie heißt „Selbsttanken" auf Englisch?
6. In welchem Bild kostet Super am wenigsten?

An einer Zapfsäule

Eine Shell-Tankstelle

Können Sie bitte das Wasser prüfen?

You may well want to use other facilities at a petrol station. Do you know what the question in the title above means? Which of these signs would you look for if you wanted the following:

1 „Ich muß meine Reifen aufpumpen."
2 „Ich fürchte, ich brauche neue Reifen."
3 „Ich habe so schmutzige Hände."
4 „Unser Auto ist innen so schmutzig."
5 „Ich muß das Kühlwasser nachfüllen."
6 „Wir brauchen neues Öl."
7 „Die Karosserie ist ganz dreckig!"
8 „Wir müssen bald ein neues Auto kaufen."

In Germany, you can carry the air pump to your car, so checking your tyre pressures is very easy.

Ein Gebrauchtwagen

Look at this advert for a second-hand car.
1 How much does the car cost?
2 About how much is that in pounds?
3 How much deposit would you have to pay?
4 For how many months would you have to pay instalments? How much would you have to pay monthly?
5 How many kilometres has the car done?

Eine Reklame für einen VW-Passat

Mit der Bahn unterwegs

Die verschiedenen Züge

Ich reise gern mit der Bahn – es ist so entspannend, aber leider auch ziemlich teuer.

The German railway network is run by **die Deutsche Bundesbahn**. The chart on the right tells you the different types of train there are.

S-Bahn: a city and commuter train.

Nahverkehrszug: a local train, stopping at all stations.

E-Zug (Eilzug): a faster train, stopping at fewer stations.

D-Zug (Durchgehender Zug): a fast train. You'll have to pay a **Zuschlag** (supplement) unless you travel at least 50 km.

Intercity: an express train linking major cities. Again, a **Zuschlag** must be paid.

TEE (Trans-Europa-Express): a train linking European cities. First class only and very expensive!

Dieser Intercity-Zug fährt durch das Rheintal.

Der neue Expreß, der mit 250 km/h Hamburg mit Frankfurt verbindet.

Am Bahnhof

When you want to buy a ticket at a station, look for signs saying **Fahrkarten** or **Fahrausweise**. Just say how many tickets you want (**einmal, zweimal,** etc), the town you are travelling to, and whether you want your ticket **einfach** (single) or **hin und zurück** (return). You may want to buy **eine Tagesrückfahrkarte**. What do you think this is? For local journeys you can buy your ticket from a machine, as in the photo below.

Ein Fahrkartenautomat

Der Fahrplan

Zeit	Zug	Richtung	Gleis
15.37	E 3012	Gelsenkirchen 16.01 – Oberhausen 16.15 – Duisburg 16.23 – Düsseldorf 16.44 – Köln 17.23 – Düren 18.08 – Aachen 18.41	21
15.40	625	Hagen 16.02 – Wt-Elberfeld 16.20 – Köln 16.51 – Bonn 17.21 – Koblenz 17.55 – Wiesbaden 18.54 – Frankfurt 19.26 – Würzburg 20.53 – Nürnberg 21.56 – Augsburg 23.10 – München-Pasing 23.36 – München 23.46 X Nürnberg	16
15.43	D 2746	BO-Langendreer 15.50 – Bochum 15.55 – Essen 16.08 – Duisburg 16.26 – Krefeld 16.43 – Mönchengladbach 17.03	7

There are two timetables displayed in German stations: a yellow one for **Abfahrt** (departure), and a white one for **Ankunft** (arrival).

Look at this excerpt from the departure timetable at the **Hauptbahnhof** (main station) in Dortmund, and answer these questions in German:

1 Was für Züge fahren zu dieser Zeit?
2 Welchen Zug mußt du nehmen, wenn du SCHNELL in Köln sein willst?
3 Wie lange dauert die Fahrt nach München?
4 Wo fährt der Zug nach Mönchengladbach ab?

In welche Richtung?

These symbols at Frankfurt Station tell you how to find various places. Should the people below go **links** (left), **rechts** (right) or **geradeaus** (straight on)?

 **A** *Ich fahre gleich mit der Straßenbahn in die Stadtmitte.*

B 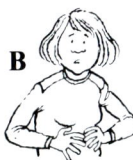 *Ich glaube, ich lasse mein Gepäck eine Stunde im Schließfach.*

 **C** *Ich habe meine Fahrkarte noch nicht gekauft.*

Ich muß unbedingt zur Post. **D**

 **E** *Ich weiß nicht, wann der nächste Zug nach Bonn fährt.*

Frankfurt Hauptbahnhof

Auf dem Bahnsteig

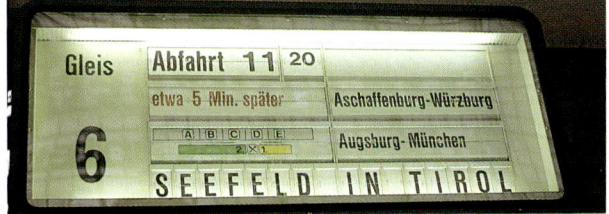

On each platform you'll find an indicator telling you the details for the next departure. What does this one tell you?
1 **Von welchem Bahnsteig fährt dieser Zug?**
2 **Wohin fährt der Zug und über welche Städte?**
3 **Was für eine Tageszeit ist es?**
4 **Fährt der Zug pünktlich ab?**

There is usually a sign on the side of the train, which tells you where it is going. To which country is the train below going? Where do you think the blue sign was photographed? What do the numbers on the bottom sign represent?

Übung macht den Meister

Imagine you are in Germany and want to visit a friend in Gladbeck. How would you ask:
1 when the next train leaves for Gladbeck?
2 when it arrives in Gladbeck?
3 from which platform it leaves?
4 what the single fare costs?
5 whether you have to pay a supplement?

Wir gehen essen

Im Restaurant

Heute gibt es viele verschiedene Restaurants in Deutschland. Es stimmt nicht, daß wir immer nur Würstchen essen.

The Germans enjoy eating out, and there is a wide range of restaurants to choose from.

The beer mat on the right shows an old hospital in the city of Nürnberg that is now a restaurant, specialising in the town's famous spicy sausages. Look at the menu below it. What is served with the sausages, and on what type of plates?

▲ *Wo in Nürnberg befindet sich das Restaurant?*

◄ *Ein kleines Restaurant in Deutschland*

Die Speisekarte, bitte

When you ask for the menu in a restaurant you say ,,**Die Speisekarte, bitte**'' or simply ,,**Die Karte, bitte**''. Often the menu is divided into sections, like those in the box below. Which name fits which drawing? An **Eintopf** is a thick vegetable soup, sometimes with a sausage or bits of meat in it. **Beilagen** are vegetables or salads to accompany a meat or fish dish.

Can you complete the names of the five soups?

Die Speisekarte			
Suppen	**Fischgerichte**	**vom Huhn**	
Eintopf	**Eierspeisen**	**Nachspeisen**	
Beilagen	**vom Kalb**	**vom Rind**	**vom Schwein**

Typische Gerichte

Germany is, of course, famous for its sausages – but that's not all the Germans eat! Especially since the arrival of the **Gastarbeiter** (foreign workers from Southern Europe), there has been an influx of Italian, Greek, Yugoslavian and Turkish restaurants and food shops.

Starters are only for special occasions and desserts are usually light. Meat dishes are very popular for the main course.

Look at the menu on the right, which shows one of the most popular meat dishes in Germany and Austria, the **Schnitzel**. It is a thin-cut, boneless piece of meat and can be pork, veal, chicken or turkey, though for the famous **Wiener Schnitzel** (the meat is dipped in a mixture of egg and breadcrumbs and then fried) it should be veal.

Sometimes a **Schnitzel** is served with a hot sauce. For example, **Zigeunerschnitzel** has a tomato and green/red pepper sauce, **Jägerschnitzel** has a mushroom sauce, and served without a sauce a **Schnitzel** is simply called **Natur**.

Another favourite dish is **Braten** (roast). Below you can see a typical German Sunday lunch: **Schweinebraten mit Salzkartoffeln, Erbsen, Möhren, Bohnen und Soße**.

You can see all these in the photo, too: **Gabel, Messer, Löffel, Untersatz, Gemüseschüssel, Deckel, Weinglas, Tischdecke**. What are they all called in English?

Using the **Speise-ABC** on page 41, work out what all the dishes on this menu are.

Mein Name ist Günter. Mein Lieblingsgericht ist Wiener Schnitzel mit Pommes frites und Salat.

Herr Ober! Fräulein!

You say „**Herr Ober!**", „**Fräulein!**" or sometimes just „**Hallo!**" to call the waiter or waitress. When you order, simply say, „**einmal**", „**zweimal**", etc. When you are ready for the bill, say „**Zahlen, bitte**" or „**Die Rechnung, bitte**".

Usually **Bedienung** (service) and **Mehrwertsteuer** (VAT) are **inbegriffen** (included). You need to check on the menu whether the prices are **Inklusivpreise/Endpreise**, or whether service and VAT are extra.

If they want to leave a tip, Germans usually round up to the next mark or two. If you want the waiter to keep the change, just say „**Das stimmt so**".

Übung macht den Meister

Imagine you are in a restaurant in Germany. How would you:
1 ask if they have a table for four people?
2 call the waiter/waitress?
3 ask for the menu?
4 order one **Schnitzel** in breadcrumbs and one chicken and chips?
5 ask for the bill?
6 tell the waiter to keep the change?

Now practise ordering items from the menu above with a partner. Take turns at being the waiter/waitress and customer.

In der Imbißstube

Was bekommt man dort zu essen?

Wenn ich nur etwas Hunger habe, esse ich am liebsten eine Bratwurst.

Eine Imbißstube in Oberursel

POMMES	1,30
FRIKADELLE	1,40
SCHASCHLIK	3,00
RIPPCHEN	4,00
½ HÄHNCHEN	4,20
SCHNITZEL	4,60
HAMBURGER	2,50
HOTDOG	2,80
CURRYWURST	2,10
BRATWURST	1,90
BOCKWURST	1,90
KARTOFFELsalat	2,00
TOMATEN „	2,20
KRAUT „	2,00
GURKEN „	2,00
BOHNEN „	2,00
NUDEL „	2,00

If you're feeling hungry, you'll find plenty of **Imbißstuben** (snack bars) and **Wurstbuden** (sausage stands) to provide you with a snack. The menu on the right is from a snack bar in **Dortmund**; you can find out what all the items are from the **Speise-ABC** opposite. French fries are served **mit Ketchup/Tunke** (tomato sauce) or **mit Mayonnaise** and with a little plastic fork. Sausages are usually served **mit Brot** or **mit Brötchen**.

Which town do the motorcyclists on the left come from? Use the chart on pages 30 and 31 to help you.

McDonalds gibt es auch...

They're never far away! How do the prices compare with those at a McDonald's near you?

Can you explain the spelling of the word **Respeckt** above? Where are there seats for 140? What do you think **Verschenk-Schecks** are?

...und viele Pizzerias...

Do you recognise all the types of pizza?

...und ab und zu einen Waffelstand!

Auf der Zeil in Frankfurt

Speise-ABC

Here is a useful list of words to help you understand menus.

Apfel(∵) – apple
Apfelmus – apple sauce
Apfelsine(-n) – orange
Aprikose(-n) – apricot
Banane(-n) – banana
Beilagen – garnishes, usually vegetables
Bier – beer
Birne(-n) – pear
Blumenkohl – cauliflower
Bockwurst(∵e) – boiled sausage, frankfurter
Bohne(-n) – bean
Braten – roast
Bratwurst(∵e) – fried sausage
Champignon(-s) – mushroom
Currywurst(∵e) – fried sausage in hot sauce
Ei(-er) – egg
Eierspeise(-n) – egg dish
Eintopf(∵e) – thick soup, stew
Eis – ice cream
Eisbein – pig's knuckle
Erbse(-n) – pea
Erdbeere(-n) – strawberry
Fanta – a fizzy orange drink
Fisch(gerichte) – fish (dishes)
Fleisch – meat
Forelle(-n) – trout
Frikadelle(-n) – meat patty
Fruchtbecher – fruit sundae
Geflügel – poultry
gemischter Salat – mixed salad
Gemüse – vegetables
Getränke – drinks
Gurke(-n) – cucumber
Hackfleisch – minced meat
Hähnchen(-) – chicken
Himbeere(-n) – raspberry
Honig – honey

Huhn(∵er) – chicken
Jägerschnitzel – thin-cut meat in mushroom sauce
Johannisbeere(-n) – redcurrant
Kakao – cocoa
Kalbfleisch – veal
Kartoffel(-n) – potato
Kartoffelpüree – mashed potatoes
Kirsche(-n) – cherry
Kloβ(∵e)/**Knödel**(-) – potato dumpling
koffeinhaltig – with caffeine
Kohl – cabbage
Kotelett – chop
Krabbe(-n) – prawn
Kräuter – herbs
Krokette(-n) – croquette potato
Lachs – salmon
Leber – liver
Limonade – fizzy drink
Linsen(suppe) – lentil (soup)
Meerrettich – horseradish
Möhre(-n) – carrot
Niere(-n) – kidney
Nudel(-n) – noodle
Nuβ(∵) – nut
Obst – fruit
Ochsenschwanz(suppe) – oxtail (soup)
Omelett(-s) – omelette
Orangensaft – orange juice
Pfannengerichte – fried dishes
Pfirsich(-e) – peach
Pilz(-e) – mushroom
Pommes frites – French fries
Pute(-n) – turkey
Reibekuchen(-) – potato fritter
Reis – rice
Rindfleisch – beef
Rippen/Rippchen – spare ribs

Rosenkohl – Brussels sprouts
Rosinenstuten – raisin bread
Rotkohl – red cabbage
Rührei(-er) – scrambled egg
Russisches Ei – egg in mayonnaise
Saft – juice
Sahne – cream
Sahneschnitzel – thin-cut meat with cream
Salat – green salad, lettuce
Salzkartoffel(-n) – boiled potato
Sardelle(-n) – anchovy
Sauerbraten – soured beef
Sauerkraut – pickled cabbage
Schaschlik – kebab
Schinken – ham
Schlagsahne – whipped cream
Schnitzel – thin-cut filleted meat
Schwarzbrot – black bread
Schweinefleisch – pork
Schweinshaxe – knuckle of pork
Senf – mustard
Soβe/Sauce – sauce, gravy
Spargel – asparagus
Spiegelei(-er) - fried egg
Suppe – soup
Thunfisch – tuna fish
Tomate(-n) – tomato
Traube(-n) – grape
Waffel(-n) – waffle
Wein – wine
Weinkraut – cabbage pickled in wine
Weintraube(-n) – grape
Wiener Schnitzel – veal fried in breadcrumbs
Wurst/Würstchen – sausage
Zigeunerschnitzel – thin-cut meat with tomato and green pepper sauce
Zwiebel(-n) – onion

Weitere Informationen

If you would like to know more about German food, send a stamped addressed envelope (large enough for a booklet 26 cm × 19 cm) to CMA UK Office, CMA House, 17A Church Road, London SW19 5EQ. They will send you their pamphlet **Food and Drink from Germany**. You can use this letter as a model:

> Aberdeen, den 18. August
>
> Sehr geehrte Damen oder Herren,
> Ich bin Schülerin an einer Schule in Schottland, wo ich Deutsch lerne. Ich würde mich sehr darüber freuen, wenn Sie mir ein Exemplar Ihrer Broschüre "Food and Drink from Germany" zuschicken könnten.
> Mit freundlichen Grüßen.
> Kitty Strachan

Ich habe so einen Hunger

Zweimal Gulaschsuppe mit Brot, bitte.

Und zweimal Rumpsteak mit Pommes frites und Salat.

Und zwei Portionen Erbsen, bitte.

Und du? Hast du keinen Hunger?

Im Café

Die Qual der Wahl

German cafés tend to be rather elegant and, therefore, quite expensive. You can sometimes get a hot snack in a café, but the emphasis is on **Kuchen, Torten und Eis** – cakes, gateaux and ice cream. The cakes are delicious, and the choice is enormous.

The cafés are often attached to a **Konditorei** (cake shop). You choose a piece of cake (**ein Stück Kuchen**) in the shop, and it will be brought to you in the café.

In einem deutschen Café: Die Qual der Wahl – welchen Kuchen soll ich nehmen?

Ein Café in Köln

You can buy both alcoholic and non-alcoholic drinks in a café. What would you order from the menu below? What does the Coke contain?

Lecker!

Diese zwei jungen Frauen haben ein Stück Mohnkuchen (poppy seed cake) bestellt.

- **Reginaris** is a type of **Mineralwasser/klarer Sprudel** (mineral water).
- **Schorle** is wine mixed with mineral water.
- **A Portion** or **Kännchen** of coffee gives you two cups.
- **Glühwein** is a hot drink made of red wine – very warming in the winter.
- **Grog** is another hot alcoholic drink. What is it made of?
- Have you noticed that tea is served in a glass, not a cup?
- **Limonade** just means fizzy drink, not lemonade. That is why the menu says **Limonade mit Zitronengeschmack**. Fizzy orange is **Orangenlimonade**!
- Some of the wide range of German cakes are: **Käsekuchen, Apfelkuchen, Erdbeertorte, Nußtorte, Obsttorte** and **Schwarzwälder Kirschtorte**. What flavours are they?

Erfrischungsgetränke

240	Glas Coca-Cola *(koffeinhaltig)*	0,2 l	1.90
250	Glas Fanta	0,2 l	1.90
261	Flasche Reginaris		1.90
270	Glas Granini Apfelsaft	0,2 l	1.90
271	Glas Granini Orangensaft	0,2 l	2.50
212	Schorle weiß	0,2 l	2.50
213	Schorle rot	0,2 l	2.50
	Für den großen Durst:		
268	Limonade mit Zitronengeschmack	0,2 l	1.—
269	Limonade mit Zitronengeschmack	0,4 l	1.90

Warme Getränke

290	Tasse Kaffee		1.80
291	Portion Kaffee		3.60
292	Tasse Kaffee entkoffeiniert		1.80
293	Glas Tee mit Milch oder Zitrone	0,2 l	3.90
210	Glühwein		4.—
211	Grog von 4 cl echtem Übersee-Rum		

Zweimal Schokoladeneis, bitte

You can buy ice cream in cafés, at stands and in ice-cream parlours. What would you order from the stand in the photo? Which fruit flavours are mentioned?

Which of the ice creams on the right looks the most tempting? Which looks the most unusual? What does **neu** mean?

Practise ordering your ice cream from this advertisement and from the stand on the left.

Spiel...Spiel...Spiel...Spiel

Copy these boxes onto paper and then fill in the missing words in German. The last letter of each word is the first letter of the next word. What is the vertical key word on the left?

1	fried sausage	11	omelette
2	plate	12	tomatoes
3	rice	13	noodle
4	soup	14	salmon
5	eggs	15	juice
6	red cabbage	16	grapes
7	lentils	17	kidney
8	nut	18	thick soup
9	steak	19	fish
10	cocoa	20	chicken

Übung macht den Meister

Imagine you are in a German café with a friend. How would you:
1 order a cup of coffee and a glass of lemon tea?
2 ask for a piece of apple cake with cream and a piece of Black Forest gateau?

Ein Straßencafé in Berlin.

Wir gehen einkaufen

Öffnungszeiten

One of the joys of visiting a foreign country is to see what is different in the shops and to buy a few souvenirs. But be careful – opening times are often different too, as you can see by the sign from a German shop (right). In the country, many shops close at lunchtime, but in big towns they usually stay open. All shops, however, close for the weekend at lunchtime on Saturdays, except on the first Saturday of the month – **der lange Samstag**. To avoid traffic congestion, some cities provide free buses to take shoppers from car parks outside the city and back.

1. Wann öffnet dieses Geschäft morgens?
2. Wann schließt es abends?
3. Wie lange hat es mittags geschlossen?
4. An welchen Tagen hat es nachmittags zu?
5. Was bedeuten die anderen zwei Schilder auf Englisch?

Wo gibt es etwas zu kaufen?

Kannst du mir helfen? Wo muß ich hin, um all diese Sachen zu kaufen?

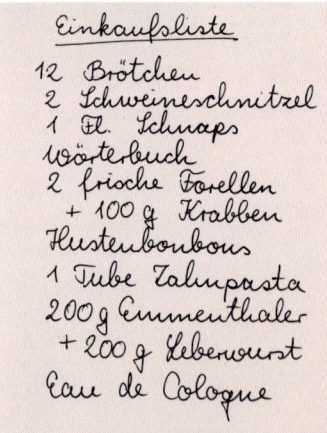

Und dann muß ich noch meine Stiefel zum Schuster bringen, meine Haare schneiden lassen und meinen Flug nach England buchen!

If you need medicines, go to an **Apotheke**. If you need toilet articles or camera supplies, go to a **Drogerie**.

Ich kaufe mir etwas zu essen

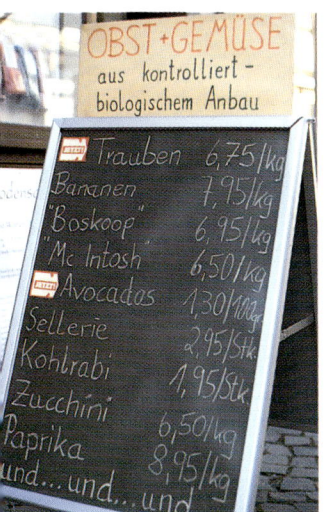

Wie heißen diese Obst- und Gemüsesorten auf Englisch? Schreib eine Liste mit den englischen und den deutschen Wörtern!

If you buy fruit or vegetables in Germany, ask for them in **Kilo** (kilograms) or in **Pfund** (pounds). **1 kg = 2 Pfund**. Yet one kilo is equivalent to 2·2 British pounds – so is a German **Pfund** heavier or lighter than a British pound? What is special about the fruit and vegetables on the left?

Übung macht den Meister

1 Practise asking each other the prices of the fruits and vegetables in the photo on the left.
2 Play out little scenes in which you order different quantities of the fruit and vegetables.

Ich sammle für mein Album

If you go to Germany, collect wrappers and labels to stick in a scrapbook like the ones below.

What is special about this ravioli and how is the sauce described?

What does this dish contain? Why might a firm call its products „Du darfst"?

What product is this wrapper taken from?

Give four reasons why this apple juice should be particularly good for you. What do we learn about the bottle?

What product was in this tin?

47

Im Kaufhaus

Auf welcher Etage?

Here are the names of some of the many big **Kaufhäuser** (department stores) you find in Germany. How many of them do you find in the UK, too?

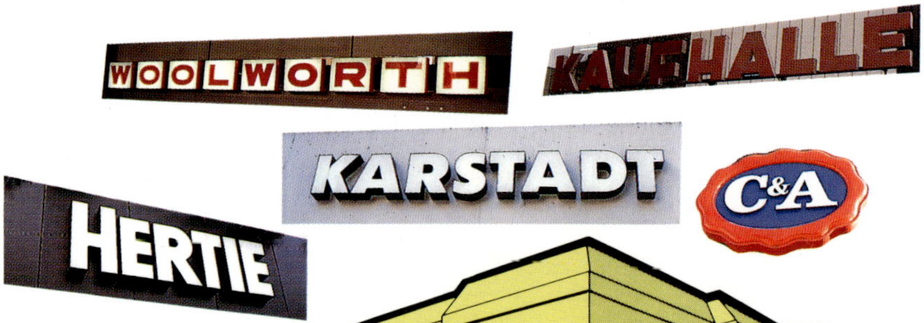

Look at this plan of the department store **Kaufhof** in Munich. Which floor do the people below need?

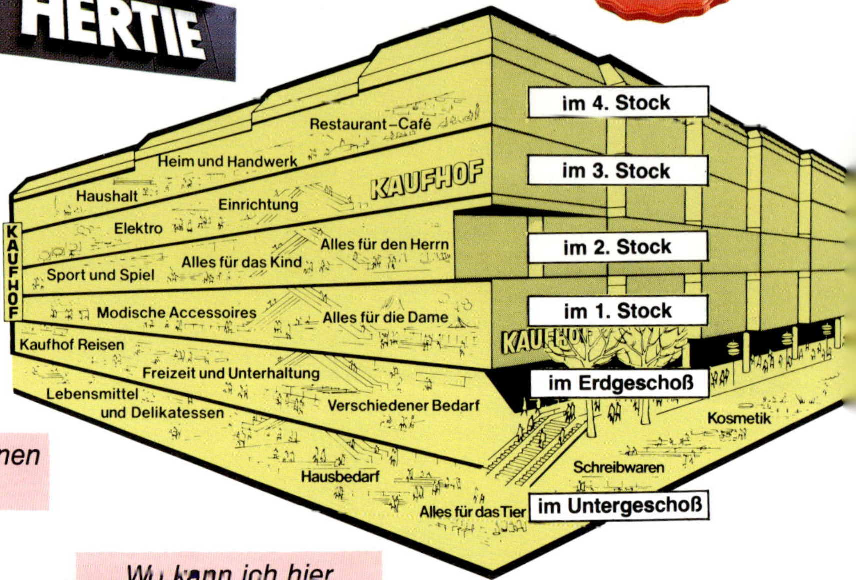

A: Wo kann ich hier einen Rasierapparat kaufen?

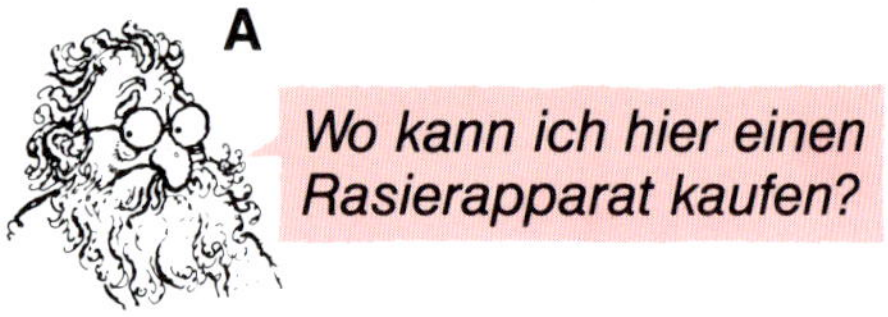

B: Wo kann ich hier einen Kamm kaufen?

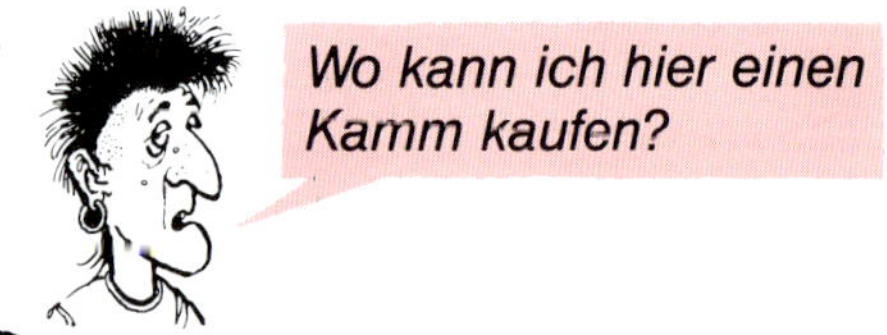

C: Wo kann ich hier Futter für meine liebe Schlange kaufen?

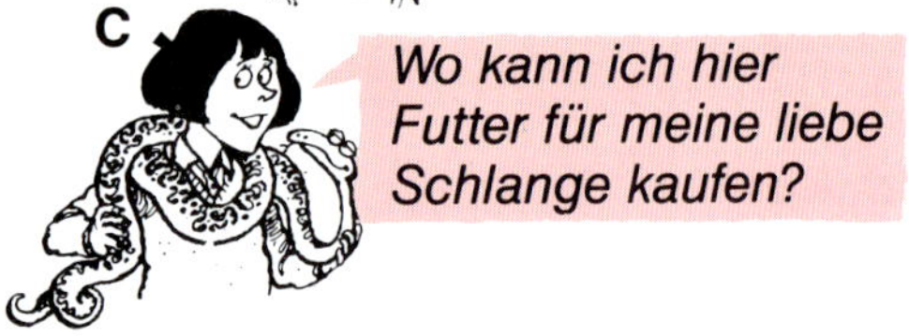

D: Wo kann ich hier Kleidung kaufen?

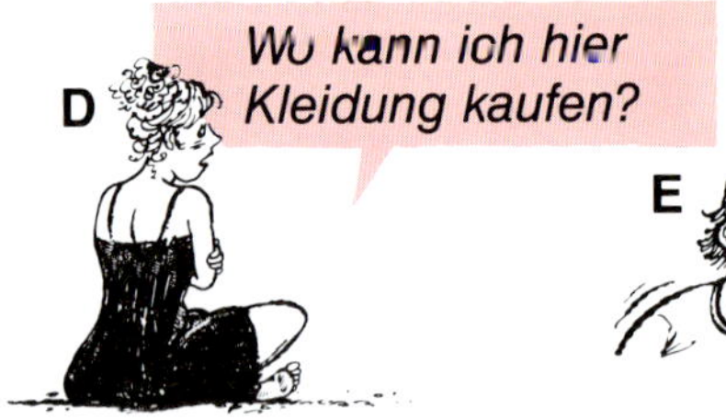

E: Wo kann ich hier etwas zu trinken bekommen?

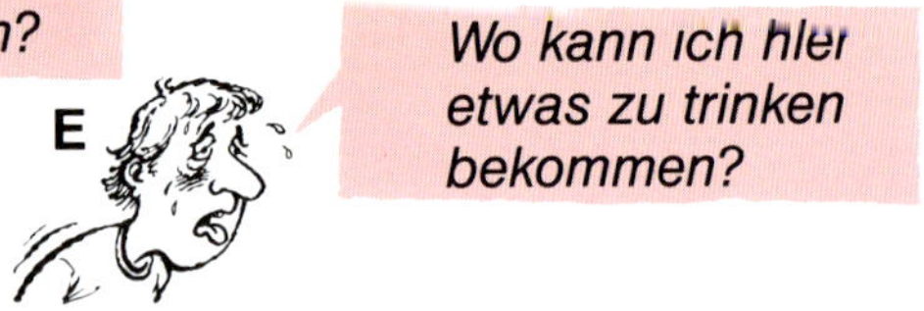

Ich brauche 'was zum Anziehen!

Kann ich diese Pullis anprobieren?

Der ist mir zu klein. Haben Sie den eine Nummer größer?

Der ist mir zu groß. Haben Sie den eine Nummer kleiner?

Der ist mir zu teuer. Haben Sie etwas Billigeres?

Die Farbe gefällt mir nicht. Haben Sie ihn in Rot?

Der gefällt mir sehr gut. Ich nehme ihn.

Wo kaufe ich am besten neue Kleidung?

 1
 2
 3

Which shop does each of these need to go in?

A Ich heirate bald.

B Ich suche eine weiße Bluse zu meinem neuen Rock.

C Ich brauche einen neuen Anzug.

D Ich kaufe mir ein neues Kleid.

 4

An der Kasse

Clothes are not too expensive in Germany and are generally good quality. Of course, you can pay a lot if you want to! For example, what do you think of these prices in a Wiesbaden boutique? Many people think Wiesbaden is the most elegant and expensive town in the country.

◀ *An der Kasse in einem Kaufhaus*

Übung macht den Meister

Imagine you are in Germany, and you want to buy a pair of trousers. How would you say the following?
1 Tell the shop assistant the colour you want and the size you need.
2 You are shown a pair. Say that you like them and ask if you can try them on.
3 Ask the price. Say they fit you but are too expensive and ask for something cheaper.
4 Ask the price of the new pair. Say you like them and that you'll take them.

Bei der Reinigung

If you are in Germany and your clothes get stained, you may need a **Reinigung** (dry cleaner). With a partner, practise asking the price of dry-cleaning various items from the list below. What do they all mean?

Was kostet es, diesen Mantel reinigen zu lassen?

Souvenirs zum Mitnehmen

Wo kann ich Souvenirs kaufen?

It's time I bought some souvenirs to take home with me!

A

B

C

D E

F

G H

If you go to Germany, Austria or Switzerland, you'll probably want to buy souvenirs for your family and friends – and for yourself, of course! But what can you buy? Maybe these shops and signs will give you some ideas.

Which shop should each of these people go to, to find what they're looking for?

1 „Ich suche ein Lederportemonnaie für meine Mutti."

2 „Ich habe mir immer Ohrringe gewünscht."

3 „Ich habe wenig Geld – ich kann mir nur ein paar Ansichtskarten leisten."

4 „Ich würde gern meinem Vater einen Bierkrug schenken; ich hoffe, daß er nicht zu teuer ist."

5 „Vielleicht gibt es hier ein kleines Spielauto für meinen Bruder."

6 „Ich wünsche mir ein süßes Kuscheltier – für mich selbst!"

7 „Aufkleber wären eine gute Idee."

8 „Vielleicht bekomme ich hier einen elektrischen Wecker."

Other suggestions would be German or Swiss chocolate or trainers. If you're really stuck for ideas, look for the **Geschenkabteilung** in a department store!

Was ist im Sonderangebot?

Of course, it's always worth looking out for special offers. What is on offer in each of these signs?

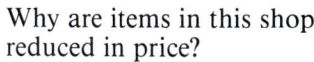

Why are items in this shop reduced in price?

The **WSV** and **SSV (Winter- und Sommerschlußverkauf)** are highlights in the German shopping year! Look at this advertisement for **Karstadt**, one of Germany's biggest stores.

1 What time does the store open?
2 How long does the sale last?
3 How can you tell which things are on sale when you are in the store?
4 What material are the handbags made of?
5 How much do fashionable dresses cost?
6 How much are the men's pyjamas?
7 What can you get for 1 DM? And for 3 DM?

Schilder im Schaufenster

Here are some signs you might see in shop windows.

A What is happening at this shop?
B What can you find inside this shop?
C What type of shop is this and what has happened?
D What do we know about this shop?
E Who is being looked for?
F What two things are forbidden?

A
D
B
E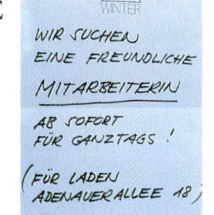
C
F

Auf der Post

Schilder am Postamt

You will often see the signs on the right outside German post offices. What do you think the second symbol represents? Anything to do with the postal system – phones, post boxes, post buses, vans – is yellow.

Inside the post office, if you want to buy stamps look for the words **Postwertzeichen** or **Briefmarken** (it often says **in kleinen Mengen** next to it – what do you think that means?). If you want to phone home, look for the sign **Ferngespräche** (long-distance calls).

What can you do at the counter below?

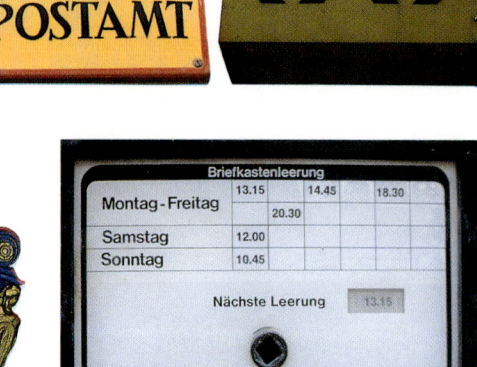

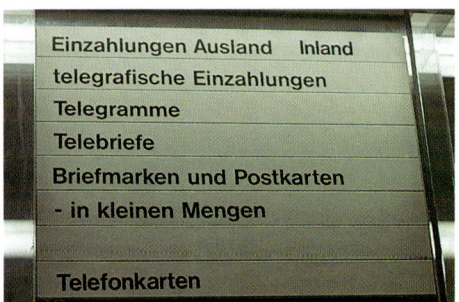

Ein Schalter im Postamt

Ein alter Briefkasten...

...und ein neuer Briefkasten

Ein Postbus in den Bergen

Look at the photo of the new post box above, and answer these questions in German.
1. Wann ist die nächste Leerung?
2. Wie viele Leerungen gibt es an einem Werktag?
3. An welchem Tag wird am frühesten geleert?
4. Wann ist die einzige Leerung am Samstag?
5. Um wieviel Uhr ist die letzte Leerung in der Woche?

 The red dot on the new post box indicates that there is a late collection.

Ruf doch mal an

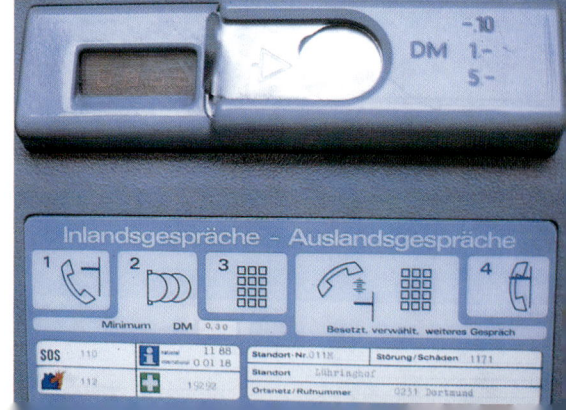

Phoning home is easy.
All you have to do is dial:
- 00 and your country code
- your area code *without the 0*
- your own number.

Die Postleitzahl

Germany, Austria and Switzerland all have a similar kind of **Postleitzahl** (post code) system. Each country is divided into numbered areas. In Germany, there are 10 main postal areas which are numbered from 0 to 9. For example, all **Postleitzahlen** in area 0 start with a zero, Dresden and its surrounding area is 01 and Leipzig is 04. A **Postleitzahl** always has five figures, for example, the **Postleitzahl** 60064 in a Frankfurt am Main address starts with **60** for the city (and its surrounding area) and ends with **064** for the location within the city.

The largest cities have more than one **Postleitzahl**. Berlin has 10, 12, 13 and 14, Hamburg 20, 21 and 22 and Munich 80 and 81.

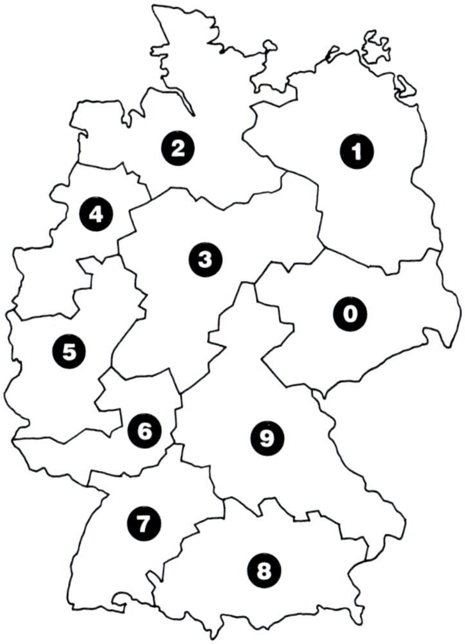

In Austria, **1**=Wien, **2**=Niederösterreich (Norden), **3**=Niederösterreich (Süden), **4**=Oberösterreich, **5**=Salzburgerland, **6**=Vorarlberg/Tirol, **7**=Burgenland, **8**=Steiermark, **9**=Kärnten.

Der Briefträger oder Postbote

Which countries do these stamps come from?

Look at the photos of the telephone on the left and the sign on the right, and answer these questions in German.
1. In welcher Stadt ist es?
2. Wo in der Stadt ist es?
3. Welche Nummer mußt du anrufen, wenn du:
   – die Polizei brauchst?
   – keine Verbindung bekommst?
   – die Feuerwehr brauchst?
4. Wie heißt „Telefonieren ohne Münzen" auf Englisch?

In der Stadt

Wie fahre ich am besten?

Ein Bus in Wiesbaden

Eine Straßenbahn in Dortmund

Die Schwebebahn in Wuppertal

Ein Berliner Doppeldeckerbus

All towns in Germany have a bus system, though Berlin is the only one to use double-deckers. Many towns still have trams – what are the advantages of trams over buses? For a bus or tram, you can buy your ticket in advance or from the driver. You then have to put it in an **Entwerter** (cancelling machine) to make it valid.

Several towns have an **U-bahn** (underground), though this often just means that the trams travel underground. Only one town, Wuppertal, has a **Schwebebahn** (monorail). The town is stretched out along a river valley; which river do you think it is? They once carried a baby elephant in the monorail to advertise the famous Wuppertal Zoo. Unfortunately, it panicked and jumped through the doors, landing (unharmed) in the river below!

Übung macht den Meister

Imagine you are in a German town and are trying to find your way to the swimming pool. How would you ask:
1 if you can get to the swimming pool by tram or bus?
2 which number you should take?
3 where you should get out?
4 where the nearest stop is?
5 how often they run?

If you were in Königstein, the pool on the right is the one you would arrive at. It's called a **Kurbad** (spa pool) because Königstein is a spa town, where people go to benefit their health. What facilities are offered at this pool?

Wer arbeitet in der Stadt?

Here are just a few of the people who work in and around the town. Can you put the missing words in their mouths? Choose from the list in the box.

Sanitäter
Müllmänner
Stadtmusikanten
Straßenverkäufer
Schornsteinfeger
Schaffner

Wir sind . . . . in Dortmund.

Die Sachen sind so billig! Ich bin . . . . in Köln.

Wir sind . . . . bei der Feuerwehr in Unna.

A

B

C

D

Wir sind...Habt ihr ein paar Mark für uns?

E

Ich bin . . . . Ich arbeite auf dem Frankfurter Hauptbahnhof.

F

Ich bin . . . Ich bringe Glück!

Wir sind auch Stadtmusikanten – aus Bremen. Habt ihr von uns gehört?

„Die Bremer Stadtmusikanten" ist ein berühmtes Märchen von den Gebrüdern Grimm.

Wo kann ich parken?

If you travel into town by car, it's important to understand the many signs you see at car parks. Which sign is being referred to in each of these statements?

1 Man darf hier nur parken, wenn man zur Apotheke geht.
2 Hier darf man nur 2 Stunden parken.
3 Ohne Parkschein darf man hier nicht parken.
4 Abends dürfen nur Frauen hier parken.
5 Hier darfst du gar nicht parken.
6 Diese Plätze sind nur für Rollstuhlfahrer.

Ein Spaziergang durch eine deutsche

Viele finden Frankfurt grau und steril – aber es ist viel los!

Now let's have a wander round one German town and look at it in more detail – Frankfurt am Main. Situated on the River Main, and with easy access to the Rhine, Frankfurt has always been an important trading town. Today, it's Germany's financial centre, containing the **Bundesbank** (Central Bank of Germany) and the **Börse** (stock exchange).

Mainansicht

Die Frankfurter Altstadt

Zwei Lokalschilder am Römerberg

We'll start our walk in the **Altstadt** on the **Römerberg**. Nearly the entire city of Frankfurt was destroyed by bombs during World War II, so what we see in the old town has been painstakingly rebuilt. Several of these old houses now contain cafes and bars, with elegant signs hanging outside. The sign on the left, above, is advertising Frankfurt's most famous drink – **Apfelwein** or **Appelwoi** as the locals call it. It's a dry apple wine, something like cider.

Auf der Zeil

Leaving the Cathedral, it's only a short stroll to the **Zeil**, once a cattle market but now the heart of the shopping centre. It was made a **Fußgängerzone** (pedestrian precinct) in 1973. One per cent of Germany's total retail trade business is done in this one street. The photo was taken just before Christmas; on a warm summer's day it's transformed into a stage for musicians, magicians and other street entertainers. There's always a food stand nearby, too, so it's easy to spend a whole day there, enjoying the shops and the entertainments.

Of course, you may want – or need! – to win some money so that you can buy some of those enticing goods in the stores. Here's the place to do it. What is the maximum prize? Can you win anything other than money?

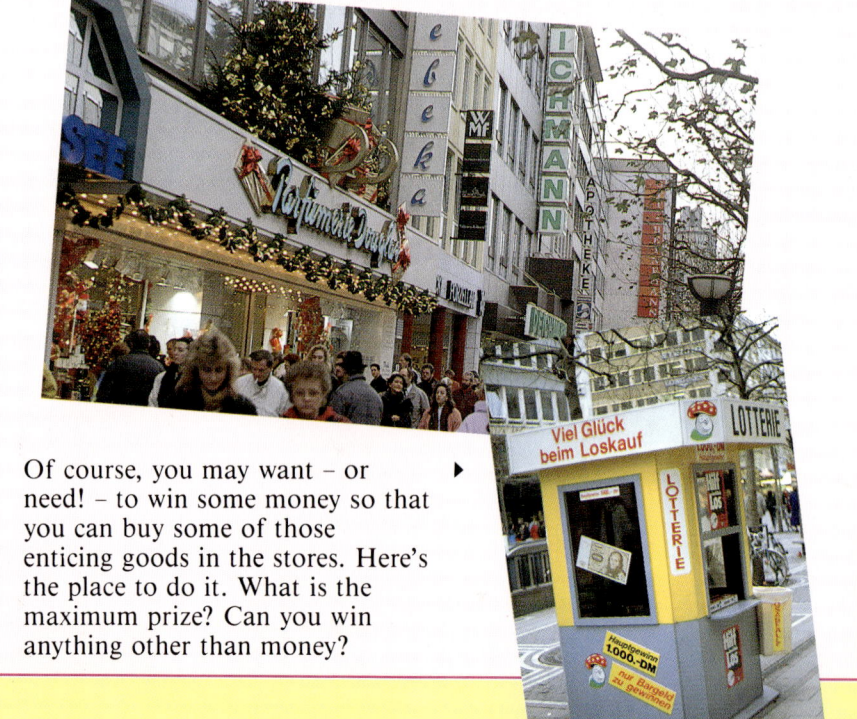

Großstadt

On the opposite side of the square stands Frankfurt's most famous historical building, the **Römer**, now the City Hall. Fifty two German kings and emperors used the **Römer** as an Imperial Hall after being crowned in the city. Today, you can still visit the **Kaisersaal**. Where does the sign tell you to go to buy tickets?

Häuserfassaden am Römerberg

Der Römer

Behind the **Römerberg** is the **Dom St. Bartholomäus**, built in the 16th century. Ten Holy Roman Emperors were crowned in this cathedral. You can get a great view from the top!

Der Frankfurter Dom

Das Bankenviertel

Now let's move on to the **Bankenviertel**, the financial heart not only of Frankfurt but of Germany itself. Here the skyline reminds you of Manhattan, to some people's delight and others' annoyance! Also in this area is the new **Messeturm**, over 200 metres tall, housing offices for the 800-year-old Frankfurt Trade Fair.

What might Goethe have to say about the tower behind him? Goethe is Germany's most famous playwright and poet and was born here in Frankfurt.

Ein typisches Hochhaus mit dem Goethedenkmal.

Tschüs, Frankfurt

There's much more we could see and do, if we had the time. There's the **Alte Oper**, a large concert hall rebuilt in the 1970s. Then there's the **Museumsufer**, a whole collection of museums by the river. There's plenty to do in the evenings, too – let's pop across the river to Sachsenhausen for a meal before going home!

Altstadt Sachsenhausen

Was gibt's zu sehen?

Im Verkehrsamt

1 Museum
2 Reiterhof
3 Fluß zum Angeln
4 Tennisplatz
5 Kunstausstellung
6 Wanderweg
7 Kegelbahn
8 Freibad
9 Flugplatz
10 Golfplatz
11 Hallenbad
12 Kinderspielplatz

When you visit a German town, the best place to go to first is the **Verkehrsamt** (tourist information office). There, you can get a street map and some information about the town and what entertainments it offers. The brochure provided by the **Verkehrsamt** in Rothenburg uses symbols to show what you can do there. Which symbol goes with which form of entertainment?

Das Rathaus

Das Rathaus und der Marktplatz in Tübingen, einer alten Universitätsstadt am Neckar

Ein Tourist versucht die Leistung des Bürgermeisters zu wiederholen.

Most towns have a **Rathaus** (town hall). In the photo above you can see two people outside the **Rathaus** in Rothenburg acting the parts of the mayor and his daughter. Every year, the city celebrates the time when the mayor's daughter begged attacking enemies not to sack the city. They agreed – provided that a citizen could drink a three-litre jug of wine in one gulp. The mayor did so!

Übung macht den Meister

Imagine you have just arrived in a German town and you go into the tourist office. How would you ask:
1 if they have a town plan?
2 if the brochures are free of charge?
3 what there is to do for young people?
4 what there is to see in the area?

Ein Stadtplan

Having acquired a town plan, can you now find your way around the town? The map on the right shows the centre of Freiburg, a beautiful university town in the **Schwarzwald** (Black Forest). Imagine you are standing on the star, facing north. With a partner, practise asking the way to various places on the map.

Entschuldigen Sie, bitte. Wie komme ich zur Universitätskirche?

Ganz einfach. Geh hier geradeaus, und nimm die erste Straße rechts. Die Kirche ist sofort auf der linken Seite.

1 Münster 2 Kaufhaus 3 Wenzingerhaus
4 Rathaus 5 Universitätskirche
6 Universität 7 Martinstor 8 Schwabentor

Verstehst du die Schilder?

You're sure to see lots of different signs when you're walking round a town. Do you know what these signs mean?

A

B

C

D

E

F

G

H

I

J

K

Habt ihr was gegen mich?

Wir bleiben zu Hause

Was kann man zu Hause machen?

Young Germans and Austrians probably have the same interests as you do. Here's what some of them said, when asked what they like to do at home.

Ich spiele sehr gern mit meinem Computer.

Ich bin eine Leseratte – Krimis lese ich am liebsten.

Und ich schreibe gern meinen Brieffreundinnen. Übrigens, wie findest du meine Banane?

If, like Martin, you enjoy reading, there's quite a range of teenage magazines you can buy. You can see some of them in the photo below, which was taken outside a kiosk in Salzburg, Austria. Which magazines might tempt you?

Vor einem Kiosk in Salzburg

Ich spiele gern mit meinen Eltern Gesellschaftsspiele, so wie Monopoly.

Of course, you can also get books out of the library. Below you can see the opening times for the central library in Dortmund.

1. An welchem Tag hat die Bücherei zu?
2. Kann man samstags die Jugendbücherei besuchen?
3. Wann macht die Bücherei morgens auf?
4. Wann kann man in der Woche die Zeitung lesen?

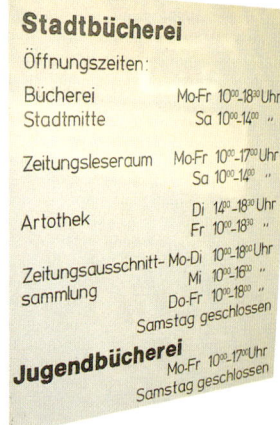

Was läuft im Fernsehen?

Television is as popular in Germany as it is in many other countries. There are three channels: **1. Programm (ARD), 2. Programm (ZDF)** and **3. Programm** which is different from region to region (**Nord, West, Hessen, Südwest, Bayern**, etc.). Many German homes now have cable TV too, which offers up to 15 channels, including three in English and two in French. Many sporting events, such as Wimbledon and some football league matches, are only shown on cable TV. Austria has only two channels but people there often tune in to German television as well.

Look at this extract showing the programmes for one of the German channels for January 1 and answer the questions in German.

1. Welches Programm is das?
2. Wie heißt der 1. Januar auf deutsch?
3. Um wieviel Uhr beginnt das Konzert aus Österreich?
4. Welche Sportart kann man sehen?
5. Wie heißt der amerikanische Film, den man abends sehen kann?
6. Wie lange dauert der Film, der kurz nach Mitternacht anfängt?
7. Wann kann man die Nachrichten sehen?
8. Welche Sendung würdest du am liebsten sehen?

And if you can't find anything you like on television, you can always go to a video shop and borrow a film.

Auszüge aus Hör zu, Deutschlands beliebtester Fernsehzeitschrift

◀ *Ein Videogeschäft in Oberursel*

Und was machst *du* gern in deiner Freizeit?

Ich reite sehr gern!

Ich boxe gern — aber nicht besonders gut.

Ich faulenze gern. Ich brauche mir keine Sorgen zu machen.

Ich sehe den ganzen Tag fern.

Ich fahre jeden Winter ski.

Wir gehen aus!

Was läuft im Kino?

Wir gehen sehr gerne ins Kino, wenn wir Zeit haben.

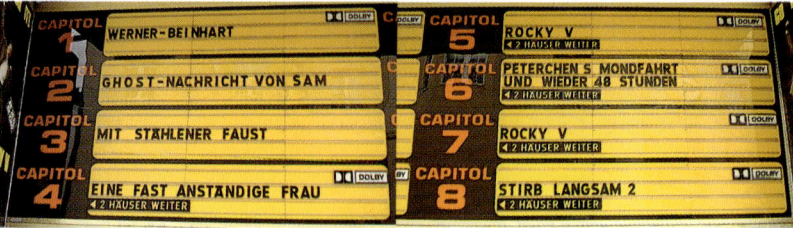

Many of the films shown in German cinemas are British or American. Do you recognise any of the films above being shown in Dortmund? See if you can find out the literal meaning of the film titles. However, the German film industry has also been very successful in recent years and some film directors, such as Wim Wenders and Volker Schlöndorff, have gained an international reputation.

Films, and other events, are often advertised on **Litfaßsäulen** (advertising columns) as in the photo on the far left.

Look at the advertisements and answer these questions in German:
1 In welchem Kino läuft *Ghost*?
2 Wann beginnt die erste Vorstellung von *Arielle – Die Meerjungfrau*?
3 An welchem Tag kann man diesen Film nicht sehen?
4 Dürfen 5-jährige diesen Film sehen?
5 Such die deutschen Wörter für (a) mermaid, (b) performance, (c) age limit, (d) news, (e) fist, (f) respectable.

Konzerte sind auch schön!

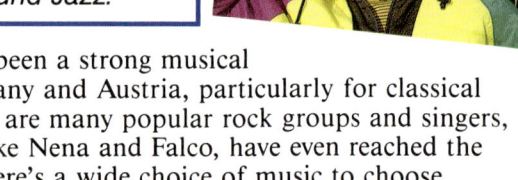

Musik ist meine Leidenschaft, besonders Rockmusik und Jazz!

There has always been a strong musical tradition in Germany and Austria, particularly for classical music. Now there are many popular rock groups and singers, some of whom, like Nena and Falco, have even reached the British charts. There's a wide choice of music to choose from, as you can see from these advertisements.

Look at the advertisements and answer these questions in German:
1 An welchem Tag kann man ein Konzert der Pet Shop Boys hören?
2 In welcher Stadt kann man Judas Priest sehen?
3 Welche deutsche Gruppe kann man in Münster sehen?
4 Wie heißt die Halle, in der man Beethovens Violinkonzert hören kann?
5 In welches Konzert würdest du am liebsten gehen?

Das aktive Leben!

Aber, wie du schon siehst, ist Sport mein anderes Hobby. Ich bin ein großer Anhänger von Borussia Dortmund.

Das Endergebnis war 0-3.

If, like Matthias, you enjoy sport, you'll enjoy yourself in Austria or Germany. They love their sport, both watching it and taking part! In the photo on the right Stuttgart have just scored against the home team, Borussia Dortmund, in a stadium specially built for the 1974 **Fußballweltmeisterschaft**.

Es ist nicht so leicht wie es aussieht!

Diese Österreicher haben gerade den Untersberg bei Salzburg bestiegen – das war anstrengend!

Windsurfen am Fuschlsee in Österreich

Ein heißer Sommertag in Leipzig – das kalte Wasser im Brunnen ist so erfrischend!

Übung macht den Meister

Imagine you are in Germany and you want to go out. You phone the organisers of different events. How would you ask:
1 what film is being shown and what time the evening performance is?
2 whether a concert is sold out and, if not, how much the tickets cost?
3 what time the swimming pool opens and closes?
4 on what day the local football team is next playing at home?

Vielen Dank für die Einladung

Kaffee und Kuchen

The Germans are very hospitable and love inviting people to their homes. If you are invited in the afternoon, it will almost inevitably be for **Kaffee und Kuchen**. The coffee is made from freshly-ground beans and the **Torten** (flans topped with fruit) and cakes are served with **Schlagsahne** (whipped cream). They look and taste delicious!

Bei diesem schönen Wetter esse ich lieber im Garten!

One area of Germany, the **Bergisches Land** near Düsseldorf, is famous for its **Kaffee und Kuchen** with a difference – bread, jam and **Quark** (curd cheese) are served as well as cakes. Can you label the things in the photo on the left with these words?

**Johannisbeerkuchen   Honig   Butter   Quark
Kondensmilch   Schwarzbrot   Zucker   Kekse
Rosinenstuten   Marmelade   Kaffee**

Schau mal – es ist so leicht, einen Apfelstrudel zu backen.

If you are invited to an Austrian home, you may well be offered **Apfelstrudel**, which is one of their specialities. It's not difficult to make and it tastes delicious. You could try making it yourself from the recipe on this tea towel.

Here Marianne, who lives in Salzburg, has stretched the dough over the table and covered it with the filling of apple, currants, sugar and cinnamon. She is now turning in the sides so that the filling doesn't fall out. Next she will make it into a long roll before putting it into the oven.

Apfelstrudel is usually eaten with cream or ice-cream and is perhaps the most famous of all Austrian pastries.

Ein Grillfest

Hier werden Schweinerippchen gegrillt.

> Wir wollen grillen!
> Wer macht mit?
>
> Wann: Freitag, den 19. Juli 20°° Uhr
> Wo : bei Matze im Garten
>   Windflügelweg 34
>
> Bringt Würstchen etc. mit und
>   vor allem
>   GUTE LAUNE!!
>
>   Matze + Björn

The Germans also enjoy barbecues and above you can see an invitation to a barbecue party. Most butchers sell meat ready spiced and marinated for a barbecue.

Look at the invitation above.
1 **Wie wollen Matze und Björn feiern?**
2 **An welchem Tag wollen sie feiern?**
3 **Wo findet der Abend statt?**
4 **Um wieviel Uhr fängt es an?**
5 **Was soll man mitnehmen?**

Eine Einladung ins Restaurant

You may be invited to a restaurant, perhaps one of a different nationality. Which countries or areas are represented below?

Ein Dankbrief

If you have been invited to Germany, you will want to write a thank-you letter when you get back home. Maybe this one from Daniel will help you.

> den 5. Januar
>
> Liebe Frau Michler,
> Lieber Herr Michler,
>
> Vielen Dank für die schöne Woche bei Ihnen. Es hat mir richtig gut gefallen. Das Essen hat so gut geschmeckt (besonders die Currywürste!), und unsere Ausflüge haben mir viel Spaß gemacht. Es war auch prima, daß Martin und ich uns so gut verstanden haben; überhaupt waren Sie alle so nett zu mir!
>
> Morgen fängt die Schule wieder an – leider!
> Schöne Grüße von meinen Eltern, meiner Schwester und natürlich von mir. Grüßen Sie bitte Martin und Caroline.
>
> Alles Gute!
>
>   Ihr
>   Daniel

So viele Schilder ...

Muß ich nach links oder rechts?

This signpost is in Schiltach in the Black Forest. What different sports can you do here? Do the people below need to go **rechts** or **links** at the signpost?

Wo sind die Toiletten?

It is important to be able to understand the signs for toilets – it could save you a lot of problems! Make sure you take some loose change with you, too, as there's often a charge.

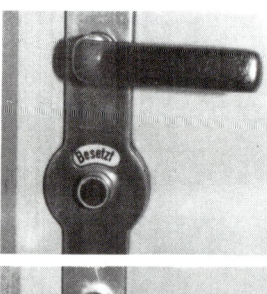

◀ Can you understand these two signs that you will find on the door?

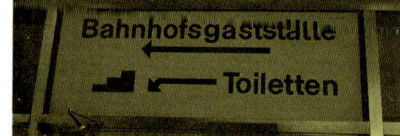

How do you get to these two toilets?

Andere Schilder an Türen und Fenstern

Here are some other signs you might see on doors or windows. What do they mean?

1. DRÜCKEN
2. ZIEHEN
3. Notausgang freihalten
4. Sind die Fenster geschlossen?
5.  AUSGANG BEI GEFAHR
6. Eingang nächste Tür ▶
7.  EINGANG AN DER ECKE

... und Reklamen!

> Die Reklamen sind wie meine Jacke – sie bringen Farbe in die Stadt!

Of course, there are lots of colourful ads, like the ones here for Coca-Cola and preserved food. In the former GDR there was virtually no advertising because goods were all made by nationalised companies, so there was no need to advertise. Instead there were many political slogans, as on the right. Times are changing now, though!

Reklamen sind überall zu finden

A ...in Schaufenstern...

B ...an Plakatwänden...

C

D ...an Bushaltestellen...

E ...auf der Straßenbahn...

F ...auf Lastern...

G ...an Litfaßsäulen...

Schau dir diese Reklamen an.
Welche ist für:
1 eine Kaffeemarke?
2 Käse?
3 einen Tierpark?
4 einen Freizeitpark?
5 Bücher?
6 ein Casino?
7 ein Milchprodukt?

As in many countries, cigarette advertisements warn about the dangers to health of smoking and indicate the quantities of nicotine and tar.

Noch mehr Schilderwald

Straßenschilder

◀ Many streets in Germany are named after famous people, places or events. What used to stand on this square in Dortmund? Who destroyed it and when?

1 Welche Person:
a) erfand die Druckerpresse?
b) war ein deutscher Dichter?
c) war Nachkriegspolitiker?
2 Welche Personen:
a) waren Komponisten?
b) begründeten den Kommunismus?

Partnerstädte

Throughout Europe, many towns are twinned (**verschwistert**) with towns in other European countries. With which town is Königstein twinned?

Dortmund is twinned with towns in seven other countries. Can you recognise the countries from the flags?

Willkommen in ▶
Königstein im
Taunus!

Paß auf!

Sometimes signs can be quite confusing — so beware!

Politische Poster

In December 1990 the first all-German elections since 1933 took place. Posters advertising the different political parties were everywhere. Here is a selection.

Does more than one party mention freedom in its poster? Which ones?
Which party's poster concentrates on the environment?

Die erfolgreiche Koalition

Die Umwelt

Wir halten die Umwelt für sehr wichtig.

Germany is extremely conscious of the many dangers to the environment and people are taught to be very **umweltfreundlich** (environmentally friendly). They are encouraged to collect their household waste according to its potential for being recycled and there are large glass and paper bins in every village and town. Motorists are encouraged to switch off their engines whenever they are stationary for a while – even at traffic lights.

Whenever plans are afoot to build on forest land, or damage the countryside in any way, there are always massive public demonstrations in opposition – which are often ultimately successful in their aim. Much cleaning-up of rivers and lakes has also taken place. The main priority now is to begin cleaning up the former GDR, a major task as the environment has been savagely neglected.

What aspects of the environment do **Die Grünen** emphasise in their poster at the top of this page?

What are you being asked to do in the signs on the right?

◀ How many languages do you recognise on this rubbish bin?

Why are different times mentioned on these paper and glass bins?

In einer deutschen Schule

Das Schulsystem

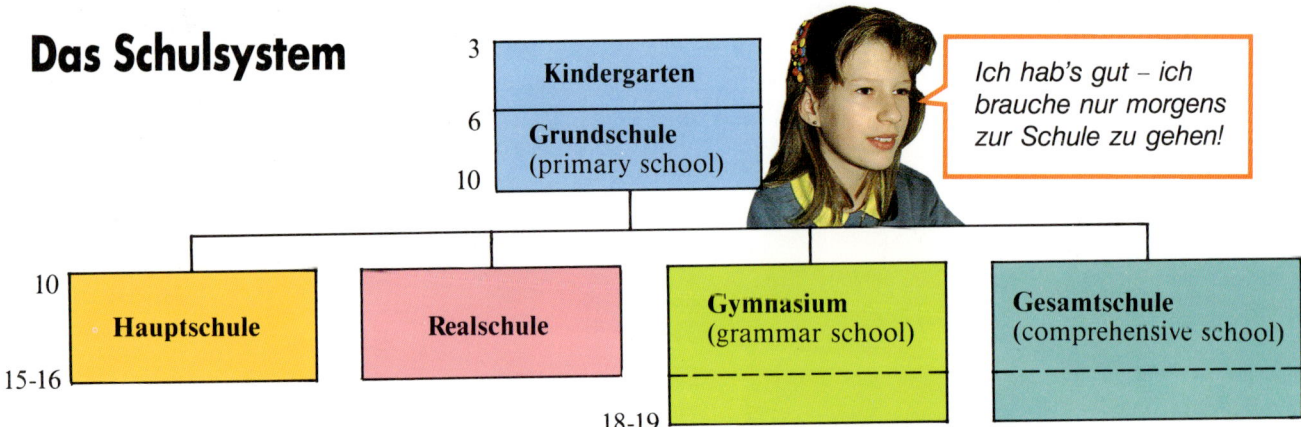

Ich hab's gut – ich brauche nur morgens zur Schule zu gehen!

The chart above shows the names of the different kinds of schools that German students attend. Do students start school at the same age as where you live? At what age do they change schools?

After leaving **Grundschule** (primary school), German students go on to secondary school. They must complete at least five years at secondary school. Most **Länder** divide their pupils according to ability when it comes to their secondary education, so there are not so many **Gesamtschulen** (comprehensive schools). The most academic pupils go to a **Gymnasium** and the least academic to a **Hauptschule**. In between these two is the **Realschule**, which usually qualifies pupils to follow more specialised business or technical careers.

What are the arguments for and against a system like this, which sends pupils to different schools according to their abilities?

Most schools begin at about 8am and finish at lunchtime, though sometimes there are afternoon classes for older students. There are no form periods – pupils go straight to their classes – though they usually have one lesson a week with their form teacher, a so-called **Klassenleiterstunde**. In most **Länder** pupils have Saturday school every other week. Classes are often not covered when a teacher is absent so pupils are sent home early or come to school later! Some **Gesamtschulen** are **Ganztagsschulen** (all-day schools) and have a **Mensa** where you can get lunch. Otherwise, schools do not provide lunch.

Der Stundenplan

Look at the timetable and answer the questions in German.
1. Hat Susanne jeden Tag 6 Stunden?
2. Welche Fächer hat sie verkürzt?
3. Wie oft hat sie in der letzten Stunde frei?
4. Was hat sie am Mittwoch in der ersten?
5. Wann hat sie Religion?
6. Wie viele Pausen hat sie?
7. Wann beginnt die letzte Stunde?
8. Wann ist die Schule normalerweise aus?

Hier ist ein typischer Stundenplan für eine Schülerin in der siebten Klasse (12-13 Jahre alt).

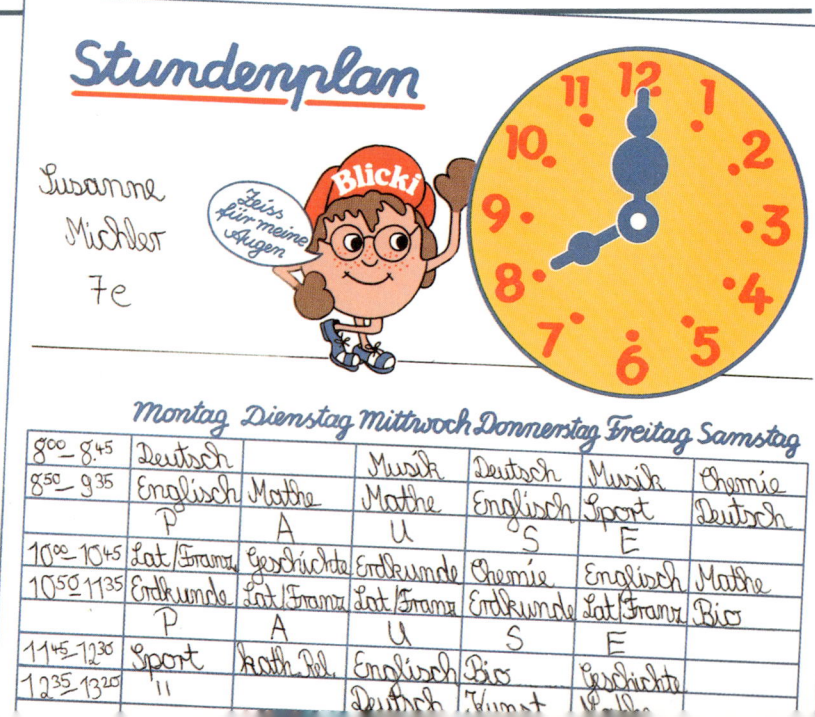

Ab in die Schule!

Tschüs, Mutti! Bis um halb zwei!

Viele Schüler fahren mit dem Rad zur Schule…

…und viele ältere Schüler fahren mit dem Mofa (ein kleines Moped) oder sogar mit dem Motorrad. Man darf schon mit 15 ein Mofa fahren und braucht keinen Führerschein.

Die jüngeren Schüler tragen einen Ranzen oder Tornister auf dem Rücken.

Das Klassenbuch

But how do they know who's absent if there's no registration?

Each class has a large book called the **Klassenbuch**. After every class the teacher enters in it what s/he has done with the class, whether anyone was absent and whether anything unusual happened, such as a major discipline problem. Teachers are not allowed to hit pupils and can only keep them in detention with the permission of the parents. The most common form of discipline is the **Strafarbeit** (extra work).

Look at the classbook extract above for a **9. Klasse**. The **e** after **Sarzio** means **entschuldigt** (excused), whilst a **Rüge** is a reprimand.

Now answer these questions:
1. How many pupils were absent this day?
2. What happened to the pupil called Espeloer?
3. Why is Bultmann mentioned?
4. Which country's economic structure was discussed in Geography?
5. In which subject was a class test given back?
6. What is the German homework and what is it presumably about?
7. Which club was held after school?
8. What was the theme of the collage done in Art?

Mehr über deutsche Schulen

Klassenarbeiten

What sort of exams do the Germans have?

„Morgen schreiben wir eine Arbeit," is the grand announcement pupils often bring home to their parents.

The **Klassenarbeiten** are written tests which are the most important factor, along with the **mündliche Note** (oral grade), in determining the **Noten** (grades) on a pupil's report. They are written in the **Hauptfächer** (core subjects) – which are German, Maths and foreign languages – while there is only the occasional **Test** in other subjects (the **Nebenfächer**). The **Klassenarbeiten** vary in length and frequency according to the age of the pupils. A 12-year-old pupil writes about eight a year, each lasting 45 minutes. A 17-year-old might only write three but each one might last three hours. They are marked on a scale of 1-6:

  1 sehr gut
  2 gut
  3 befriedigend
  4 ausreichend
  5 mangelhaft
  6 ungenügend

Grades 1-4 are a pass, grades 5 and 6 are a failure! Two 5s or 6s on a report can mean having to repeat the whole year (known as **sitzenbleiben**).

Zeugnisse

German pupils receive a report at the end of each **Halbjahr** – in February and in the summer. The report only contains grades; there are no comments about the pupil's efforts or personality.

The most important grades in a pupil's life are those on the **Abiturzeugnis**. **Abitur** (in Austria, **Matura**) is equivalent to our A-levels and decides whether a pupil goes on to further education. Pupils who leave school at 15 or 16 receive an **Abschlußzeugnis** (final report) with their final grades on it. They still have to attend a vocational school (for example, a **Berufsschule**) once a week when they start working or learning a trade.

Look at Matthias' report and answer these questions in German:
1 Wie heißt Matthias mit Nachnamen?
2 Was für eine Schule besucht er?
3 In welcher Stadt ist die Schule?
4 In welcher Klasse ist Matthias?
5 Was sind seine besten Fächer?
6 Welches Fach hat er nicht bestanden?
7 Muß er sitzenbleiben?

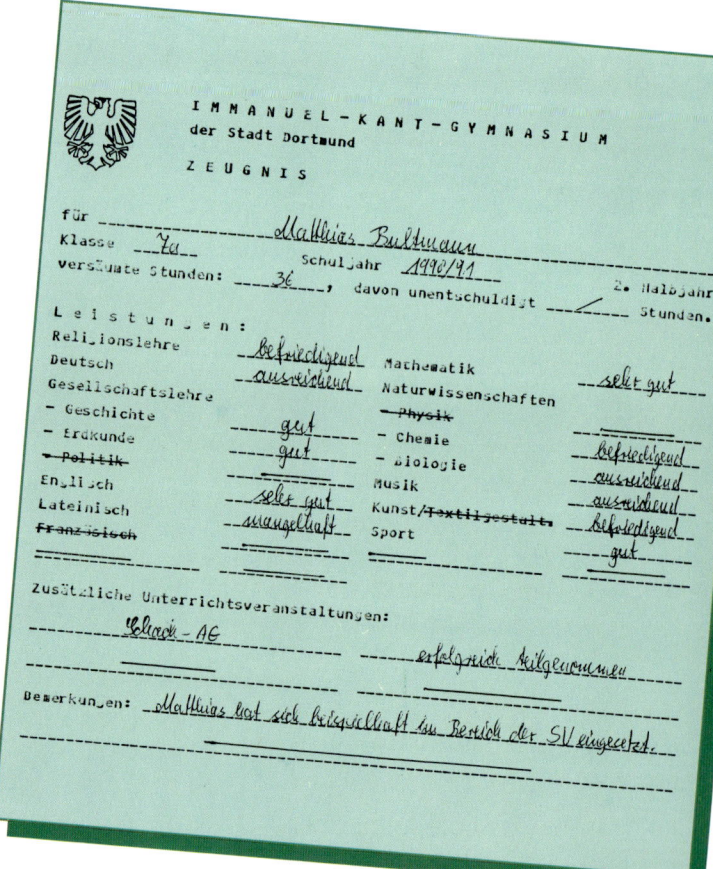

Matthias' Zeugnis

Was ist auch anders als bei uns?

Die Schultüte
On their very first day at school, children are given a **Schultüte** full of sweets.

Ein deutsches Mädchen mit ihrer Schultüte

Wandertag
At least once a year each class has a **Wandertag** (hiking day). With their **Klassenlehrer(in)** (class teacher) they go for a long walk in the country, visit a zoo or some other form of entertainment. They usually take a picnic with them.

◀ *Diese Schüler bekommen Fahrradunterricht. Später müssen sie alle eine Prüfung machen.*

▲ *Diese Klasse hört einen Vortrag von einem Förster über den deutschen Wald.*

Anagrams – Anagrams –
Unscramble the names of the six objects in the drawing.

THEF	MURDERMAGII
CHUB	LUKI
NELLIA	FISTIBELT

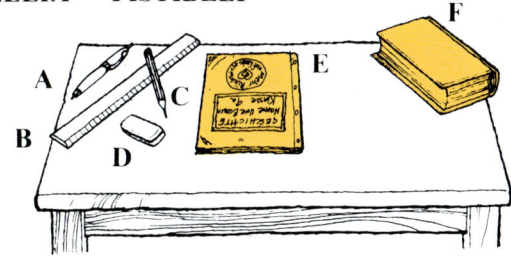

Can you unscramble these school subjects?
1. SCHINGLE
2. PROST
3. STUNK
4. GICHECHEST
5. PSYKHI
6. MAKETIMHAT
7. CHUSTED
8. BIGLOOIE
9. MICHEE
10. DEERDUNK

Übung macht den Meister

You have just arrived at a German school. How would you ask a pupil:
1. how many pupils go to the school?
2. what sports s/he plays?
3. what her/his favourite subject is?
4. what subjects s/he does not like?
5. how much homework s/he gets?

Ich habe immer so viel auf!

Hilfe!

Beim Arzt

Vergiß nicht, einen Krankenschein zu holen, bevor du zum Arzt gehst.

Health care is paid for through medical insurance. Visitors to Germany need to have their own health insurance or check if there is a special arrangement between Germany and their own country. If you need to see a doctor, collect receipts for any payments you make.

Make sure you go to the right doctor – many of them specialise in one area of medicine. Which doctor should each of these people below go to?

 1 *Ich habe einen Husten.*

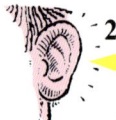 2 *Ich habe solche Ohrenschmerzen.*

3 *Mein Schwanz ist überfahren worden!*

 *Aua – ich habe furchtbare Zahnschmerzen.*

4  *Ich fürchte, ich brauche eine Zahnspange!*

5 *Ich muß meine Augen untersuchen lassen.* 6

The doctor's nameplate outside the surgery also tells you the doctor's consulting times. The nameplate on the right is Austrian – you can tell because the doctor's title is different from the German doctors' shown in the photos above. There are two other differences of language, too:

Austrian	German
Ordination	Sprechstunden
rückwärts	hinten

„Eingang rückwärts." Does that mean I have to walk in backwards?

Was ist los?

Ich habe solche Halsschmerzen.

Magenschmerzen habe ich auch.

Und ich habe Fieber. Und mein Kopf tut so weh.

Und ich bin so erkältet.

Ansonsten geht's mir gut!

Notdienste

If you get a **Rezept** (prescription) from the doctor, take it to the **Apotheke**. If the chemist's is shut, the sign outside will tell you which one is on emergency standby. What do you think **Notdienst**, **Rezepteinwurf** and **Nachtglocke** mean?

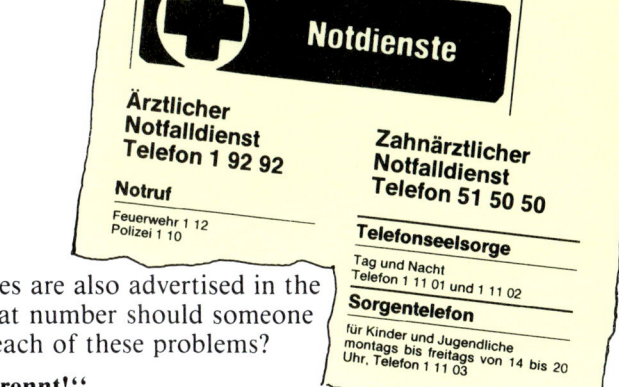

Emergency services are also advertised in the daily papers. What number should someone call if they have each of these problems?

1 „Unser Haus brennt!"
2 „Die Oma ist die Treppe runtergefallen!"
3 „Ich bin 15 Jahre alt und bin von zu Hause weggelaufen."
4 „Jemand ist bei uns eingebrochen!"
5 „Ich bin gefallen und habe mir zwei Zähne abgebrochen!"
6 „Ich fühle mich so allein. Ich bin über 80 und möchte mit jemand sprechen."

Verstehst du die Hinweise?

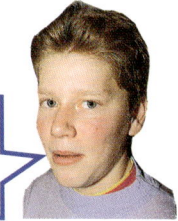

Guten Tag. Haben Sie etwas gegen Durchfall und Grippe?

This is how to ask for medicines at a chemist's. And you'll need to make sure you understand the instructions!

What are the instructions on these four medicines?

„Ich hab' mein Herz in Heidelberg verloren!"

This is the first line of a popular old German song. What does it mean?

If you've lost anything else of value, go to the **Polizeiwache** (police station) or **Fundbüro** (lost property office).

If you lose your passport, you'll need to be able to say, „**Entschuldigen Sie, bitte. Ich habe meinen Paß verloren!**" Practise saying that you have lost the six things below.

Was haben diese drei liegenlassen?

1 *Entschuldigen Sie, bitte. Habe ich meinen Regenschirm hier liegenlassen?*

2 *Entschuldigung! Habe ich meine Brieftasche hier liegenlassen?*

3 *Entschuldigen Sie! Habe ich meine Handschuhe hier liegenlassen?*

Pressemeldungen

Die Schlagzeilen

You can learn a lot of German by reading German newspapers, even if it's only the headlines. See how well you can understand these headlines, by answering the questions:
1. Which building in Leipzig is crumbling?
2. What happened in Athens?
3. How has the weather changed since yesterday?
4. Why is the Atlantic mentioned?
5. What is special about the 200 Mark notes in East Westphalia?
6. What is happening to bank interest rates?
7. What happened to the Japanese balloonist?
8. What happened to 11 people in a house?

Leipziger Rathaus bröckelt

Gefälschte 200-DM-Scheine in Ostwestfalen

Elf Menschen aus einem brennenden Haus gerettet

Suche aus der Luft nach 58 Besatzungsmitgliedern geht weiter
Zwei Schiffe im Atlantik vermißt

Sparkassen: Zinsen gehen rauf

Athen: Vier Tote bei Straßenschlacht

Japan: Ballonfahrer bezahlt Abenteuer mit dem Leben

Gestern Jahrhundert-Wärme: Jetzt kommt Kälte

Berühmte Deutsche in den Schlagzeilen

Am 3. Oktober bei der Feier zur deutschen Wiedervereinigung. Von links nach rechts: Hans-Dietrich Genscher (der deutsche Außenminister); Helmut Kohl (der deutsche Bundeskanzler) und seine Frau Hannelore; Richard von Weizsäcker (der deutsche Bundespräsident).

Kurt Masur – Dirigent des Leipziger Gewandhausorchesters, ab 1991 der New Yorker Philharmoniker.

Welche Sportler sind in den Schlagzeilen?

Here are just a few of the many famous German-speaking sports stars. Which other ones have you heard of? People who used to compete for the GDR (like Katrin Krabbe) now compete for the united Germany. Matthias Sammer was the first footballer from the GDR to play in the new German national team.

Wer ist in der Hitparade?

Look at this record chart from the magazine „Bravo".
- Wie viele von den Liedern kennst du?
- Wie viele werden von deutschen Sängerinnen/Sängern und Gruppen gesungen?
- Wie viele sind Platten aus den USA oder Großbritannien?
- Was ist dein Lieblingslied in dieser Hitparade?

Katrin Krabbe aus der ehemaligen DDR – eine der schnellsten Frauen Europas.

Lothar Matthäus – Kapitän der erfolgreichen deutschen Fußballmannschaft bei der Weltmeisterschaft 1990 in Italien.

Franz Heinzer aus der Schweiz beim Gewinn der Abfahrt bei der Skiweltmeisterschaft 1991.

Bernhard Langer – einer der besten Golfspieler des letzten Jahrzehnts.

Steffi Graf – jahrelang die Weltranglisten–Nummer 1.

#	Title	Artist
1	Sadeness – part 1	Enigma
2	Ice Ice Baby	Vanilla Ice
3	Beinhart	Torfrock
4	Pray	M C Hammer
5	Mary had a little Boy	Snap
6	I've been thinking...	Londonbeat
7	The Joker	Steve Miller Band
8	Keep on running	Milli Vanilli
9	Unchained Melody	Righteous Brothers
10	I'm your Baby tonight	Whitney Houston
11	It's a Shame	Monie Love
12	Hello Africa	Dr. Alban feat. Leila K.
13	Being boring	Pet Shop Boys
14	Real Sadeness II	After One
15	Tom's Diner	DNA feat. Suzanne Vega
16	Don't worry	Kim Appleby
17	What Time is Love	KLF
18	Show me Heaven	Maria McKee
19	So hard	Pet Shop Boys
20	How I miss you so	P.M. Sampson
21	Crying in the Rain	a-ha
22	To love somebody	Jimmy Somerville
23	Cult of Snap	Snap
24	A better Love	Londonbeat
25	It takes two	Rod Stewart & Tina Turner
26	I'll be your Baby tonight	Robert Palmer & UB 40
27	Thunderstruck	AC/DC
28	Nah Neh Nah	Vaya con Dios
29	Crazy for you	David Hasselhoff
30	Unbelievable	E.M.F.

Letzte Eindrücke

Finally Daniel's visit to Germany has come to an end. It is time to say goodbye to the family he has stayed with.

I'm back home now, but I had a wonderful time in Germany. It's great to be able to look back and remind myself of all the things I saw and did, as well as the people I met.

When you go to Germany, it's a good idea to put all your photos and things you've collected into a scrapbook. Arrange them as a diary, a day-to-day account of everything you did or saw. Or divide them into sections, like food and travel. Here is a selection of impressions from Daniel's scrapbook, which he wrote while he was still in Germany — with a little help from his friends!

Dieses Poster fand ich sehr beeindruckend.

In Frankfurt sind einige Tretboot gefahren.

In Oberursel war ich auf einem Fest. Dieses Popkonzert war klasse.

Unser Besuch in Dachau, wo es in der Nazizeit ein großes Konzentrationslager gab, hat mich sehr mitgenommen. Dieses Denkmal soll daran erinnern, daß so etwas nie wieder passieren darf.

Besonders aufregend fand ich unseren Besuch auf einer Burg, wo man Falken und Adler fliegen ließ.

Zweimal habe ich Sport getrieben. Einmal haben wir mit den Mädchen Fußball gespielt....

....und einmal habe ich Minigolf gespielt. Ich war hoffnungslos!

Das sind zwei meiner Lieblingsfotos – der Blick vom Frankfurter Dom und das Heidelberger Schloß.

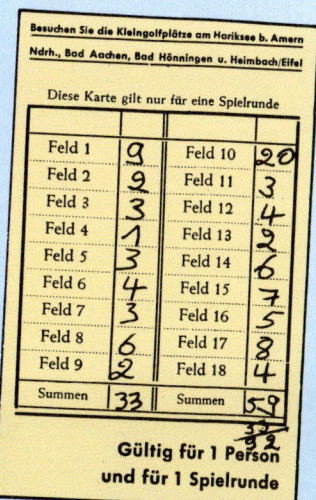

Es ist Zeit, „Auf Wiedersehen" zu sagen. Ich hoffe, daß du bald nach Deutschland kommen kannst. Es lohnt sich!

Tschüs auch von mir. Komm mich irgendwann mal besuchen!

Alles Guetä! Uf Wiederluege!

Mach's gut! Pfüat di!